THE CHURCH OF IREL
KILLALA & ACHONRY, 1870–1940

Maynooth Studies in Local History

GENERAL EDITOR   Raymond Gillespie

This pamphlet is one of eight new additions to the Maynooth Studies in Local History series in 1999. Like their twenty predecessors, most are based on theses submitted for the M.A. in Local History at National University of Ireland, Maynooth. The pamphlets are not concerned primarily with the portrayal of the history of 'particular places'. All are local in their focus but that localisation is determined not by administrative boundaries but rather the limits of the experience of everyday life in the regions of Ireland over time. In some of these works the local experience is of a single individual while in others social, occupational or religious groups form the primary focus of enquiry.

The results of these enquiries into the shaping of local societies in the past emphasises, again, the diversity of the Irish historical experience. Ranging across problems of economic disaster, political transformation, rural unrest and religious tension, these works show how such problems were grounded in the realities of everyday life in local communities. The responses to such challenges varied from region to region, each place coping with problems in its own way, determined by its historical evolution and contemporary constraints.

The result of such investigations can only increase our awareness of the complexity of Ireland's historical evolution. Each work, in its own right, is also a significant contribution to our understanding of how specific Irish communities have developed in all their richness and diversity. In all, they demonstrate the vibrancy and challenging nature of local history.

Maynooth Studies in Local History: Number 24

The Church of Ireland Community of Killala & Achonry, 1870–1940

Miriam Moffitt

IRISH ACADEMIC PRESS

DUBLIN • PORTLAND, OR

First published in 1999 by
IRISH ACADEMIC PRESS
44, Northumberland Road, Dublin 4, Ireland
and in the United States of America by
IRISH ACADEMIC PRESS
c/o ISBS, 5804 NE Hassalo Street, Portland, OR 97213.

website: www.iap.ie

British Library Cataloguing in Publication Data
Moffitt, Miriam
  The Church of Ireland Community of Killala and Achonry (1870–1940). –
  (Maynooth studies in local history; 24)
  1. Church of Ireland – History 2. Parishes – Ireland – Killala – History 3. Parishes
  – Ireland – Achonry – History
  I. Title
  283.4'172

  ISBN 0716526824

Library of Congress Cataloging-in-Publication Data
Moffitt, Miriam.
  The Church of Ireland Community of Killala and Achonry (1870–1940)
      p.   cm. — (Maynooth studies in local history: no. 24)
  Includes bibliographical references and index.
    ISBN 0–7165–2682–4 (pbk.)
    1. Church of Ireland. Diocese of Killala and Achonry—History—19th century.
  2. Sligo (Ireland: County)—Social conditions—19th century. 3. Mayo (Ireland:
  County)—Social conditions—19th century. 4. Church of Ireland. Diocese of
  Killala and Achonry—History—20th century. 5. Sligo (Ireland: County)—Social
  conditions—20th century. 6. Mayo (Ireland: County)—Social conditions—
  20th century. 7. Sligo (Ireland: County)—Religion—Economic aspects. I. Title.
  II. Series.
  BX5505. K54M64 1999
  283'. 4172—dc21
                                                                  99–30887
                                                                       CIP

Typeset in 10 pt on 12 pt Bembo by
Carrigboy Typesetting Services, County Cork
Printed by ColourBooks Ltd, Dublin

Contents

Acknowledgements

I would like to express my gratitude for the assistance received in the preparation of this study. Firstly to Dr. Jacqueline Hill and Dr. Raymond Gillespie, Dept. of Modern History, N.U.I. Maynooth for their help, interest and encouragement. Thanks is also due to Rev. Doris Clements, Tubbercurry for her valued opinions, to Raymond Refaussé and Mrs Heather Smith for their assistance in the R.C.B. library, Dublin, to Rev. R. McCarthy for the use of the Diocesan Library, Galway and to the staff of the National Archives, National Library and the Valuation Office for their help, patience and courtesy. Finally, and especially, to my husband and three children for allowing me the time and space to complete this study and for going without meals for two years.

NOTE ON TERMINOLOGY

Throughout this book, the term Protestant is used to signify members of the Church of Ireland. When other Protestant denominations such as Presbyterian or Methodist are referred to, they are identified by name. In this study, where an unqualified term of Protestant is used, it may be presumed to refer to the Church of Ireland.

1. The diocese of Killala and Achonry

6

Introduction

The united diocese of Killala and Achonry provides an excellent opportunity to study the workings of rural parishes of the Church of Ireland from the time of disestablishment of the church in 1869 up to the early years of the Irish Free State. The last bishop of Achonry, Cormac O'Coyne, died in 1561 and these dioceses have been united since 1622. St. Patrick's cathedral in Killala was reconstructed in the late seventeenth century, during the episcopate of Thomas Otway. St. Crumnathy's cathedral in Achonry, in contrast, was built by the board of first fruits in 1823, replacing a ruinous older building on the same site. It was closed and deconsecrated in January 1998. The united diocese was not wealthy, in areas it was particularly poor. The isolation of the see of Killala and Achonry and its inaccessibility, owing to the poor roads coupled with large tracts of either boggy or mountainous land, must have deterred many clergymen from serving in the area. Most bishops who were appointed to the diocese used the appointment as a stepping stone in their careers. It is not, and never has been, an important diocese, in terms of church politics.

The diocese of Killala and Achonry provides a good example of a self-contained Church of Ireland population. From 1870 to 1940 census data suggests that very few Protestants moved into the area. Changes in population occurred as a result of emigration from the area. In this region the in-migration of Protestants in the seventeenth century seems to account for a significant, stable Protestant population by 1870, whereas efforts at converting the native Irish were largely unsuccessful in this part of the country.

The Protestant population of this area was always a tiny minority. In 1871, the total population of the diocese was 186,250 persons of which 7,352 or 3.9 per cent were members of the Church of Ireland. By 1941 the Church of Ireland population had fallen to 2,473 and the Catholic population to 101,419. This represented a decrease of 66.4 per cent among Protestants and 45.6 per cent among Catholics. This drastic decrease in the number of Protestants occurred as a result of social and economic forces and resulted in the amalgamation of parishes and the closure of churches and schools. The factors which contributed to the demographic trends of this minority rural population form the focus for this study.

The people of north Mayo and south and west Sligo lived primarily on the land. The bulk of agriculture was grazing, of both cattle and sheep. Tillage was rare, owing mostly to the poor nature of the land. Near the sea, some people could augment their incomes by fishing, but an analysis of the 1901 census returns reveals that there were no Protestant fishermen in the diocese although some Protestants were involved in fishing industries and wholesaling. In spite of this there was very little industry, some attempts were made in the seventeenth and eighteenth centuries to introduce flax growing and linen weaving but this floundered. With the exception of Ballina, the only commercially significant town, the population was entirely rural and dependent on agriculture for survival, although some industries were established in Ballysadare and Collooney. Farming has always been a struggle in this area. In 1870, holdings were small and family sizes were large. Most of the area was designated as congested and between 1870 and 1940 most of the landed classes sold out to the Congested Districts Board or to the Land Commission. This had serious consequences for the viability of the Church of Ireland, since the majority of the relatively wealthy landowners had been members of the church, contributing a large portion of its income. After their departure, the church had to muster support from the less well off parishioners. Following the foundation of the Irish Free State, another exodus of the wealthier members of the Church of Ireland occurred and only those parishes that had sufficient middle income parishioners survived and in a few instances churches were obliged to close.

History is almost always written by the victor, and in the case of the history of Southern Ireland 1870–1940, this has meant by Roman Catholics. The indisputable plight of Catholic peasants, living in miserable hovels and exploited to sustain exorbitant lifestyles of the Protestant aristocracy, is the picture presented to us in most history books written prior to 1970 as being typical of all Catholics. Not all Catholics peasants lived in such extreme conditions, there was a considerable Catholic middle class who enjoyed a better lifestyle, as well as some landlords. Almost every area of the country has a tradition of reasonably well off Catholic families as well as the poorer peasants. Just as all Catholics were not miserable peasants, not all Protestants were from the landed classes. There was a significant body of Protestants who did not belong to the landlord or aristocratic or even professional classes, being either tenant farmers, merchants or tradesmen. These persons were neither fish nor fowl; they were neither Catholic tenants nor Protestant landowners. They probably had more in common with their Catholic counterparts, but both communities were prevented by their clergy and by vested interests from intermingling. The church urged vigilance against situations which might possibly lead to mixed marriages. A letter to the *Church of Ireland Gazette* from Rev. A. Sweetman, Ballinamore in 1923, advised that:

> where parents are rigid Protestants and quickly check undesirable company keeping on behalf of their growing up boys and girls, and where the clergy and their immediate connection have not transgressed on the side of leniency themselves, there are seldom any perversions to Rome.[1]

It seems that unless a clergyman is backed up by his people and that a balance of sexes preserved by importation of Protestant employees, there can be one end . . . laisser faire will accomplish nothing but extinction.[2]

The process of segregated education, the lengths to which each church went to prevent intermarriage, the feeling of superiority *vis à vis* Catholics which was bred into Protestant children, all went to produce a type of Protestant;

who – one might think – would have more in common with the Catholics of the same class than with the gentry, yet he was persuaded to regard Home Rule as a calamity and to throw his support behind the landlords in a effort to preserve the union.

The ordinary Protestants backed their leaders because, in the last resort, a Protestant clerk felt closer to a Protestant gentleman than to a Catholic clerk. He felt closer because he shared with the gentleman two basic differences from all their Catholic fellow citizens: a different concept of religion and a different concept of nationality.[3]

Throughout the seventy years in question, the rights and opinions of southern Protestants were often ignored as indeed were the Protestants themselves. One widely acclaimed textbook, the *Oxford illustrated history of Ireland* contains the following, astonishing sentence 'Partition had practical appeal to every party but one, the vulnerable and confused Catholic population of Northern Ireland'.[4] What about the southern Protestants? Were they really so insignificant a community to not even merit consideration? In order to show that the Protestant perspective was sometimes different from that commonly found in textbooks, it is useful to view the events of the years 1870–1940 as they were perceived by Protestants and by Catholics.

Seen through Protestant eyes, the years 1870–1940 were a succession of humiliations. First to occur was the forced disestablishment of their church in 1870. Shortly after, there followed the land war and accompanying crime and then the threat of home rule. Protestants saw their privileges shared with Catholics in an effort to 'kill home rule with kindness.' They perceived that their dominance in national politics had been taken from them by the passing of the parliamentary voters act (Ireland) in 1850, and after the passing of the local authority act of 1898, they were no longer the people of power in local politics. They also had to cope with increased involvement of Catholics in the professions, and for the first time found themselves in competition with the Catholic majority for positions. In the opinion of many Protestants, boards of poor law guardians were biased against them.[5] In the deanery of Claremorris the Roman Catholic clergy passed a motion asking the local district council to ignore any application for a vacancy that was not accompanied by a recommendation from the parish priest. The district council duly passed the motion, effectively keeping Protestants out of all local authority positions.[6] This increased representation of Catholics was resented by Protestants, some of whom felt that the Catholics were not of their calibre. The emergence of this new breed of Catholic politician (and businessman) was a threat to their status quo.

> In the south and west of our land, the successful shopkeeper and publican – for he invariably pursues both callings – is the centre of all movements in local politics. The landlord has been deposed but the shopkeeper has set up in his place. The poor and ignorant peasant is in his debt. The shopkeeper is a Justice of the Peace, a district or county councillor. Moreover, his sons are officials, old age pension officers, rate collectors and the like . . . Can home rule drive corruption and dishonesty from the public life of Ireland?[7]

In the early years of the twentieth century, following the land acts of 1903 and 1909, the landlords had to come to terms with the not always voluntary sale of their lands. The boycottings and intimidations of previous decades, frequently directed against them, recommenced. Protestants also saw that the United Irish League often organised, by fair means and foul, that Catholics became the owner-occupiers of lands previously held by Protestants. And still the threat of home rule would not go away. In the opinion of many Protestants, these Catholics would never be satisfied, even after all that had been granted to them.

The Protestants of the south spoke against breaking the link with Britain, but their opinion was unheeded. After 1922 the exodus of the 'servants of the realm', such as coastguards, and the Royal Irish Constabulary greatly diminished the church population, although the 'native' church population remained reasonably constant. The sense of threat and impotence in the face of the new regime was manifest in the non-involvement of Protestants in public affairs during the first years of the Irish Free State.[8] They frequently adopted an attitude well explained by Dean Griffin of 'keep your head down and avoid controversy'.[9] In some areas of the country, there was widespread intimidation. This extended to the Killala/Achonry diocese.[10] By the outset of 1922 most Protestants were resigned to the formation of the Irish Free State. They may not have agreed with it, but as the *Church of Ireland Gazette* stated 'They believed that the welfare of the country was involved in the Union. Now that the Union is gone, they are prepared to accept the decision taken against them and to support a lawfully constituted authority'.[11] With the establishment of the Free State, the Protestant community felt more isolated from the affairs of state than ever before. The victimisation of Protestants in the early days of the Irish Free State persuaded many to move to Northern Ireland, or to emigrate. Those who remained became, of necessity, a silent minority who kept to themselves. After the truce of 30 April 1923, the year passed by more peacefully but Protestants still felt insecure and unwanted in their environment. The Killala diocesan synod of November 1923 noted:

Many of our friends have left the diocese to seek homes elsewhere ... it may be, in happier times, some of them will return to us. Our sympathy goes out today to those who have suffered, as so many have, cruel and grievous loss. We are members of Church of Ireland, true to our name ... and we claim it as our right that we be allowed to live our lives in peace and security.

In 1926, it was stated in the *Church of Ireland Gazette* that the dáil contained only a handful of members whose opinions were worth listening to.[12] The coming to power of Éamon de Valera in 1932 and the passing of his constitution in 1937 was the cause of real concern to Protestants fearing the undue influence of the Roman Catholic church and its clergy in the running of the country.

It would appear that local authorities were under pressure not to employ Protestants. The Local Appointments Commission was established in an attempt to deal with the widespread corruption associated with the granting of local government appointments. The country's most celebrated case occurred in County Mayo in 1930, when the county council refused to ratify the appointment of Miss Letitia Dunbar Harrison as librarian. The council claimed that this was on account of her not understanding Irish, but undeniably, it was because she was a Protestant.[13] The *Catholic Standard* stated that 'Catholic Ireland will make short work of these Protestants who resent the desire of Catholics to live the full Catholic faith.'[14] The fears of the Protestant community were expressed in the *Church of Ireland Gazette*:

> the action of the Mayo Library Committee in refusing to appoint as librarian, Miss Letitia Dunbar Harrison, must inevitably increase the apprehensions which are felt by many as to the treatment which Protestants are likely to receive, if certain elements in the Free State get their way.[15]

The Roman Catholic archbishop of Tuam, openly stated his view that

> it is gratifying to see how the representatives of our Catholic people are unwilling to subsidise libraries not under Catholic control ... Only a thoroughly educated Catholic man or woman, loyal to and energetic in the cause of Catholic action, can be deemed fit for the highly responsible and influential post of County Librarian.[16]

The standard of Irish of Ellen Burke, the candidate proposed by Mayo county council, and backed by the Catholic church, was praised by Dean D'Alton, a prominent member of the local Catholic clergy. In fact, Miss Burke had previously been rejected by two completely different boards, on account of having failed the Irish test. However, she had the benefit of belonging to 'very respectable stock, and her people have been tried when Irish hearts and parents had to bear a good deal.' After the appointment of Miss Dunbar Harrison, the libraries all over the county were urged to close and to return their books to Castlebar. Eventually the Local Appointments Commission offered an alternative position to Miss Dunbar Harrison, who reluctantly accepted. The next librarian appointed was a Catholic.[17]

When George Coulter, a long-lived parishioner of Skreen died in 1902, an account of his life, which is essentially an account of the life of the Church of Ireland, was given in the *Church of Ireland Gazette* of 2 May 1902.

> Mr. George Coulter, one of the most notable laymen of the parish and district of Skreen, in the diocese of Killala, has passed away at the patriarchal age of 95. Born in January 1807, Mr. Coulter's long span has witnessed many and great changes – social, economic, political and religious. He lived in the reigns of five sovereigns, George III, George IV, William IV, Victoria and Edward VII. He has seen the fierce disputes on the tithe question, had witnessed the rise and fall of O'Connell, Butt, Parnell; had listened to the persuasions of Father Mathew of total abstinence fame; had seen the changes brought about by the abolition of the corn laws and the establishment of Free Trade in these countries; had seen the effects of the land legislation of Mr. Gladstone; had experienced the changes brought about by the disestablishment and disendowment of our Church; had sat under the teaching of eleven rectors of Skreen, and had seen curates come and go until he lost count of them. Independently of the great age to which he attained, Mr. Coulter was in many respects a remarkable man. He was the oldest parish clerk in Ireland, if not in the British Isles, having held that office for an unprecedented length of more than seventy years.

This obituary tells us as much by its omissions as by its inclusions. The writer makes absolutely no reference to the great Famine of 1845–47, at which time George Coulter would have been in his forties, and, in his capacity as parish clerk, should have had some awareness of the wretchedness of the region and possibly had some involvement in relief work (the population of Skreen fell from 4,103 to 2,953, during the decade 1841–51). The effects of the second famine of 1879 were also felt very severely in the region. It is unlikely that either famine made no impact on Protestants.

An elderly Protestant, in the 1940s, looking back at the years 1870–1940, would have had much cause for resentment, at the loss of privilege, power (both political and economic), land and social status. Instead of living in a country where Protestants ruled Catholics, and where the Protestant machine of state guaranteed him a living, he now lived in a situation where Protestants were ruled and, on occasions only barely tolerated, by Catholics, where local government positions, for years the livelihood of second sons, were granted preferentially to Catholics and where the Catholic clergy seemed to dictate the laws of the country.

From a Catholic viewpoint, the years 1870–1940 were very different. The nineteenth century saw the establishment of a political life for Roman

Catholics. For rural Catholics, the most important achievements were the right to vote and the right to hold leases on their farms. This increasing number of Catholic voters greatly diminished the influence of the Protestant population of Counties Mayo and Sligo.

By 1870, the elected M.P.s for County Mayo were Lord George Bingham (Conservative) and G.H. Moore (Liberal); those for County Sligo were Denis Maurice O'Connor (Liberal,) and Sir Robert Gore Booth, Bt. (Conservative). This was the first example of the influence of Catholic emancipation on the politics of the area. O'Connor was the first Catholic member of parliament to sit for County Sligo. Prior to his election, all M.P.s elected for County Sligo, without exception, were Protestant, were large landowners in the region, and most were Conservative. In 1884, the electorate was greatly increased under the 'mud cabin' reform act. After this year political representation was exclusively nationalist and Catholic. By 1890 parliamentary representation was exclusively the domain of Roman Catholics, the influence of the Protestant population of Killala and Achonry in national politics had disappeared.

In the area of tenant right, Gladstone's land acts of 1870, 1881, and 1882 gave tenants a recognised interest in their holdings and a right to a judicial rent. These benefits were the direct results of tenant agitation and of the increased influence of Catholics in politics.[18] They gave rise to a new found confidence, which when combined with a greater degree of literacy and a wider availability of reading material in the nationalist vein,[19] led to the reinforcing of the Catholic middle class who were educated and ready to take over the running of the country, both at local level by means of the boards of poor law guardians, and at national level. Home rule was the initial goal of the emerging Catholic political body. The support of the Catholic church for the movement was almost inevitable[20] and both the home rule movement and the Land League went from strength to strength. After the demise of Charles Stewart Parnell, the Land League went into a temporary decline, but was revived in the form of the United Irish League. In April 1911, a third Home Rule Bill was introduced, the goal of the nationalists was in sight. The bill was rushed through parliament in 1914, on the condition that it would not come into operation until after the war.

During the years of the war, maybe because of, and maybe in spite of the disastrous rising of 1916, Sinn Féin had become a formidable force. It was evident by 1918 that the demand was for more than home rule, in fact for total independence and in 1919 the first Dáil Éireann was summoned. The following three years saw the establishment of the Irish Free State (with partition) and the Civil War which followed it. After the cease-fire in 1923, the country tried to put itself together. By now, the government of the country was exclusively in the hands of nationalists. As the years progressed, a system of party politics emerged in which few Protestants felt inclined to participate.

This study is composed of four sections. The first section deals with the Protestant population. Where did they live? Why did they live in some areas and not in others? What they did they work at? Were they native to the area or transient residents? What were their housing conditions? How did their numbers and age of marriage compare with their Roman Catholic neighbours? How many children did they have? How did these factors compare with the behaviour of the Catholic population? If they were farmers, what size and valuation was their farm? What methods of farming did they employ? Did they remain after the creation of the Irish Free State? Did the following generation remain or did they emigrate?

The next part deals with the financial viability of the diocese. What impact did disestablishment of the church have on its viability? To what extent were church finances dependent on the landed classes? Could the church survive after the dissolution of the estates in the early twentieth century? Why did some parishes survive while others did not? What impact did the creation of the Irish Free State have on the viability of the church?

The following chapter deals with the provision of education, the transition from schools run under the auspices of the various bible societies to state funded schools and the distribution of Protestant schools. Were these schools attended by Roman Catholic children? Did they remain open for the duration of the study or did declining numbers force them to close? Where were the children of the landed classes educated? What happened in areas where there was insufficient Protestant children to maintain a school? What about secondary education?

The final chapter deals with the degree to which the Protestant and Catholics communities integrated with each other. What was the attitude towards Protestant children in Catholic schools? How were children of Roman Catholic and Presbyterian families treated in Church of Ireland schools? Was there any evidence of proseltisym? What was the attitude to mixed marriages? Did Protestant tenant farmers take part in the land war? Was there any evidence of intimidation towards Protestants during the division of the estates in the early years of the twentieth century? Did any Protestants support home rule? What were their feelings after 1922?

In this study, I will attempt to shed light on the 'small' Protestants, who rented or owned possibly under a hundred acres of mediocre land, who supported their local church and sent their children to the local Protestant national school but could not afford to send them to secondary school unless they won a scholarship. This study does not examine the minutiae of parish life, the church fetes, lantern lectures, missions, Sunday school outings, temperance societies. Instead it provides a statistical and analytical understanding of the impact of social and economic forces on a sparsely populated minority church.

The Church of Ireland Community

This chapter deals with the persons who comprised the Church of Ireland community of the united diocese of Killala and Achonry from 1870–1940. It will show that the Protestant community in the Killala/Achonry diocese was concentrated in certain parishes and was unusual in that it was made up of poor Protestants, mostly farmers occupying farms of c. 50 acres. Undeniably they were better off than most of their Catholic neighbours but when compared to Protestants elsewhere in the country it is evident that they were not wealthy. In 1967, when Donogh O'Malley was establishing the scheme to provide free secondary education, the delegations from the Protestant community in Sligo stressed that they were unlike the rural Protestants from elsewhere in Ireland, they claimed that they were poor Protestants.[1]

The Protestant population in 1870 varied widely from parish to parish. Some parishes had a high density of Church of Ireland parishioners, others had virtually none.[2] Pockets of Protestants occurred around Ballysadare, Collooney, Ballymote and Tubbercurry, around Killala, Ballina, Mullafarry and Ballycastle, around Skreen, Dromard and Dromore West, and around Easky, Kilglass, and Castleconnor. Other areas, such as Swinford, Charlestown or Kiltimagh never had any significant Protestant presence. In order to explain this divergence, it is necessary to look before the period of study to see what factors influenced the settling of Protestants in the area.

County Sligo or the Tyrawley barony of County Mayo were not included in the Cromwellian transplantation of the 1650s. County Sligo and Tyrawley was earmarked for Cromwell's own soldiers.[3] Very little of this land was returned to Catholic landowners after the restoration. This will be referred to as the 'plantation area'. At the end of Charles II's reign, over 90 per cent of the county was owned by Protestants. In the mid-eighteenth century Protestant weavers were brought in from the north of the country, to establish a linen industry. Lord Shelbourne introduced a colony of weavers and settled them in Ballymote. Arthur Young, who visited Sligo in 1776, gave an account of this colonisation.[4] He wrote that the O'Haras of Annaghmore had built houses on their estate for eighty such weavers and that Mr. Fitzmaurice had done the same in Ballymote, stating that the enterprise started badly but later got on its feet:

> Each weaver was provided with a cottage, half a rood of land for a potato garden, and grass for a cow, thus affording him the means of subsistence for his family without allowing his time or thoughts to be

distracted from his main business by the details of a small farm . . . The manufacture of unions, a mixed fabric of linen and cotton has been introduced, and is carried on extensively.[5]

This immigration of northerners may also explain the significant Presbyterian presence in Ballymote where a Presbyterian church still exists. By the end of the eighteenth century linen had become the chief manufacture of the county and there was a linen hall in Sligo town. Although it is not in the diocese, this town was very important to the residents of the diocese, socially, educationally and economically.

There was an attempt at a linen industry in the Tyrawley barony of County Mayo at Ballysakeery when Lord Arran introduced northern weavers to that region. The industry floundered, but the northerners remained. We can conclude therefore, that the creation of a linen industry was probably significant to the enlargement of a Protestant population, which survived considerably better than the industry.

Another motive for the introduction of Protestant tenants or workers was the effect of this increased Protestant population on the outcome of elections. In 1768, the octennial act was passed, which ensured elections at intervals of eight years or less. This compelled members of parliament to attend more closely to their county influence. This affected the religious composition of the community because the elective franchise was confined exclusively to Protestants. The rationale for this was explained by Rev. Seymour:

> From this it naturally resulted that every gentleman of property, who was ambitious of county influence, either for the election of himself or the election of his friends, was necessitated to promote Protestantism among his tenantry. A Popish tenantry could not vote, could not strengthen his position at election, and became a dead weight on his hands; while a Protestant tenantry, by being able to vote in their capacity of Protestant freeholders, became an object of desire to all country gentlemen.[6]

The majority of landlords in County Sligo were resident and were involved in local parish affairs. Their presence in the area, together with their patronage of church and schools, strengthened the position of the Church of Ireland in the diocese. The importation of Protestants in the form of Cromwellian soldiers, northern weavers, and sundry Church of Ireland voting tenants, ensured a significant Church of Ireland population in those parishes of the united diocese that are within County Sligo. The most easterly parishes of County Sligo, Ballysadare, Emlyfad (Ballymote) and Killaraght (Gurteen)[7] were targeted by the evangelicals during the period of the second reformation in the mid-nineteenth century. The curate of Ballysadare during the 1840s was William Newton Guinness, a protégé of the strongly evangelical Archbishop

Trench. In Ballymote, Rev. John Garrett was the evangelical clergyman in this parish and together with his son, Rev. John jnr., they spent over a hundred years as rectors of the parish. Edward Powell, the clergyman of Killaraght during the early 1800s, was a close friend of Archbishop Trench. Even more interesting is the location of the Church of Ireland families in Killaraght. According to the 1901 census, nine households, out of a total of twenty-one Church of Ireland households, were located on lands that had formerly been owned by Lord Lorton, of Rockingham, near Boyle. This gentleman was well known for importing Church of Ireland tenantry onto his estate. This also occurred on his lands in Counties Longford and Leitrim. A similar situation is found in the Tyrawley barony of County Mayo, where Cromwellian officers such as Sir Arthur Gore and Sir Edward Ormsby received estates but in other areas of County Mayo such as Kilconduff (Swinford) and Castlemore (Ballaghaderreen) the situation was completely different.

There was a strong history of linen manufacture in west Mayo, in the late eighteenth century. This was concentrated around three centres, Westport (Knappagh), Castlebar and Turlough but all were in the adjacent diocese of Tuam. The Protestant population of Mayo, excluding Tyrawley, was largely made up of persons who belonged to the landed classes and persons who were not native to the area and were employed by the landed classes such as game-keepers, butlers, estate managers, mill managers, persons employed as public servants, such as coastguards, and R.I.C. men for instance.

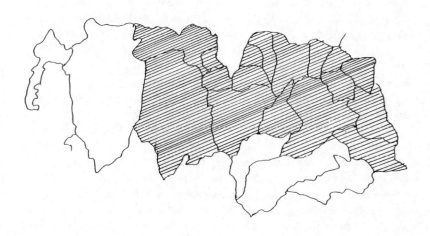

2. Areas of land granted to Cromwellian soldiers

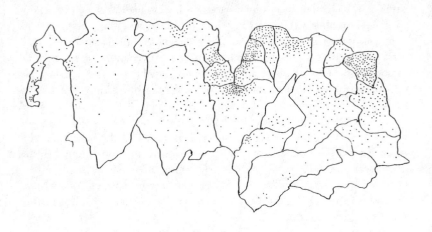

3. Distribution of Church of Ireland households in 1901. Each dot
represents a Church of Ireland household.

During the first half of the nineteenth century, missionary societies had
been very active in the Erris region of the diocese. They established mission
stations in the parishes of Kilcommon Erris and Kilmore Erris, at Belmullet,
Binghamstown, Ballycroy, Poulathomas, and Bangor Erris where they built
churches and schools. In 1870 the Protestant population of the parishes of
Kilcommon Erris and Kilmore Erris was composed of persons directly employed
by the mission and whose presence in North West Mayo related directly to the
presence of a mission station, persons whose parents or grandparents had been
Catholics and who had changed their faith in the early nineteenth century, or
by persons associated with the coastguard or lighthouse services. Other
parishes, where missionary societies had not been active, such as Castlemore,
Kilconduff, had even fewer Protestants and as these were inland parishes they
had no coastguard influence.

In this isolated part of Mayo, few landlords were resident on their estates,
few had any allegiance to the area and most quickly availed of the land acts to
unload their already over-mortgaged properties. In Sligo, however, more
landlords were resident, and though these also sold their estates, more of the
landlords in County Sligo and in Tyrawley remained in the region afterwards.

The disestablishment of the Church of Ireland, shortly followed by the
speedy exodus of the landed class and their accompanying entourage, followed
then by the departure of the 'servants of the crown', all undermined the
foundations of the Church of Ireland in the Killala and Achonry diocese, and
the creation of the Irish Free State caused the departure of even more

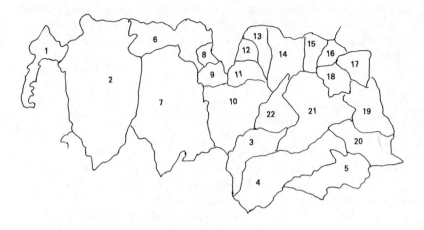

4. The parishes of the diocese in 1870.

KEY TO FIGURE 4.

County Mayo
(excl. Tyrawley)
1 Kilmore Erris
2 Kilcommon Erris
3 Straide
4 Kilconduff
5 Castlemore

County Mayo (Tyrawley)
6 Dunfeeney
7 Crossmolina
8 Killala
9 Ballysakeery
10 Kilmoremoy

County Sligo
11 Castleconnor
12 Kilglass
13 Easky
14 Kilmacshalgan
15 Skreen
16 Dromard
17 Ballysadare
18 Killoran
19 Emlyfad
20 Killaraght
21 Achonry
22 Kilmacteigue

Protestants. The result of this was the demise of some parishes where there was little or no indigenous, long standing Protestant population, and the survival of those parishes where there was a sufficient number of established, middle income parishioners to maintain a parish, without external support. In parishes such as Kilcommon Erris (Belmullet), after the departure of the coastguards and the landed classes, the only remaining church people were those who had converted earlier in the century and were now left isolated, without any parish infrastructure. Added to this sense of isolation was the remaining legacy of animosity towards Protestants and especially towards those associated with missionary societies. The number of persons involved was so small, in 1941 there were four persons in Poulathomas and seven in Kilmore Erris (Binghamstown), that the churches in these regions were not viable. Indeed, these regions only ever had 'imported' church populations and as such were artificial parishes.

Another very important factor in determining the fate of a parish, was the size of the population at the outset. As can be seen in table 1, the population of Ballysakeery fell by 161 persons between 1883 and 1941 and the Protestant population of Kilcommon Erris fell by approximately the same amount (155). However Ballysakeery still had 156 Protestants in 1941 whereas only twelve Protestants lived in Kilcommon Erris at the end of the period of study. A parish with 156 parishioners had a need for a clergyman, church and school, although, for financial reasons, it was forced to merge with Killala in 1926. Kilcommon Erris, with its twelve parishioners, could not function as a parish. The Protestant population was too small to retain a separate identity. It merged with Kilmore Erris in 1926 and with Crossmolina in 1933.

Constraints of space do not permit an analysis of each constituent parish of the diocese but it is worth examining the decline in population of the three neighbouring parishes of Castlemore (Ballaghaderreen), Killaraght (Gurteen) and Emlyfad (Ballymote) as a case study. Castlemore parish in County Mayo never had a significant local Protestant presence. The local landlords, the Dillons, were very pro-Catholic. Killaraght in County Sligo, on the other hand, had landlords who were strongly Protestant, but who were not resident, and consequently were not involved in church affairs at local level, although they did support the church financially. Emlyfad's Protestant population in County Sligo had been augmented directly by the introduction of northern

Table 1. Parish populations, 1883 and 1941.

Killala Diocese	1883	1941	decrease	% dec	Achonry Diocese	1883	1941	decrease	% dec
Ballysakeery	317	156	161	50.8	Achonry	120	30	90	75.0
Casleconnor	267	105	162	60.7	Ballysadare	624	175	226	59.3
Crossmolina	479	165	314	65.6	Collooney	381	155	226	59.3
Dromard	129	65	64	49.6	Emlyfad	565	110	455	80.5
Dunfeeney	280	60	220	78.6	Kilconduff	81	9	72	88.9
Easky	376	110	266	70.7	Killaraght	171	25	146	85.4
Kilcommon Erris	167	12	155	92.8	Killoran	618	270	348	56.3
Kilglass	250	105	145	58.0	Kilmacteigue	91	32	59	64.8
Killalaq	204	44	160	78.4	Straid	176	35	141	80.1
Kilmacshalgan	552	180	372	67.4	Tubbercurry	466	145	321	68.9
Kilmoremoy	908	150	758	83.5					
Kilmore Erris	198	7	191	96.5	Total	3293	968	2307	70.1
Poulathomas	10	3	7	70.0					
Skreen	336	160	176	52.4					
Total	4473	1322	3151	70.4					

Reports of the Diocesan Synods, 1883 and 1941, in R.C.B. library, Dublin.

Protestants[8] and the local landlords, who were mainly resident, involved themselves in the daily life of the parish. It also must be recognised that, whatever
the percentage decrease in population, there is a point below which a parish
is not viable.

The percentage decrease in Protestant population in Emlyfad (55.3 per
cent) was not significantly less than that in Castlemore (65.4 per cent) and
Killaraght (60.9 per cent). However, the actual population in Castlemore
(thirty seven persons in 1911) was insufficient to justify the maintenance of
a church and seventy parishioners in Killaraght in 1911 could neither justify
nor maintain a parish. Emlyfad also experienced a serious decline in population but in 1911 there were 250 Church of Ireland persons still resident in the
parish, thus ensuring its continuance. An entry in a new preacher's book of
Emlyfad parish, which was begun on 7 January 1908 states:[9]

> The former preachers book was begun in 1889, the 1st. Sunday after
> Easter, the morning congregation was 130, evening 65. During the
> interval 22 whole families have emigrated, including 2 that migrated and
> at this date the sale of Earlsfield involves the loss of another family,
> without anybody to take their place.
>
> J. Gordon Walker,
> Dean of Achonry, Ballymote, April 1910.

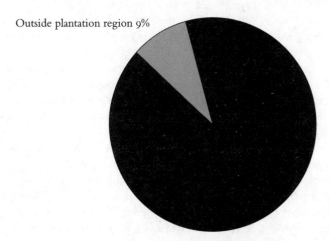

Outside plantation region 9%

Inside plantation region 91%

5. Location of the Church of Ireland Population in 1901.

As already explained, some parishes had no indigenous Church of Ireland population, composed of families who generation after generation lived and worked in the parish. In a rural, farming community, it is safe to presume that farming Protestants were indigenous, whereas labourers, R.I.C. men, teachers, factory workers may have been more mobile and consequently more likely to leave the region. Parishes outside the plantation region consistently showed a lower percentage of farmers, the majority of families located there not having a long-term attachment to the area. In contrast, inside the plantation region, the majority of households derived their living from the land, and as such were more likely to remain in the region. Appendix 1 lists the number of Protestant farming families in the diocese in 1901.

Another variable that yielded information on the potential viability of parishes was the place of birth of a parish population. For the purpose of this study, persons born in Counties Mayo, Sligo and Roscommon were considered to be indigenous, or native, persons born outside these three counties were considered to be 'blow-ins' and less likely to remain in the region than those who had been born in the area. As was expected, the parishes within the plantation region had a high native population (80.53 per cent) compared to those parishes which were dependent on migrant or transient parishioners (51.7 per cent).

The effect of the presence of coastguards, recruited from the British navy, in the diocese was considerable. These persons were almost exclusively British, Protestant and married with young children. An analysis of the 1901 census shows that in some parishes they contributed a large proportion of the congregation, as in Kilmore Erris where they accounted for 64 persons out of a total of 109, or 58 per cent of the Church of Ireland population. Until 1922, individual families came and went from the coastguard stations around the coastal parishes, but their replacements were always persons from the same background, age and religion, so that they effectively comprised part of the permanent community. Their sudden departure after 1922 left some parishes with seriously diminished congregations. This was especially felt by school managers as the presence of a coastguard station virtually ensured the main-tenance of the parish school.[10] The removal of ten to twenty children from small schools of this type was disastrous for the future functioning of the parish. Parishes which, in 1901, appeared to have a significant church popu-lation, became non-viable after the departure of the coastguards.

A comparison of the 1901 census returns of the union of Kilmore/ Kilcommon Erris (Belmullet and Binghamstown) and Kilmacshalgan (Dromore West) verifies all the previous claims. The presence of thirty-three farming families in Kilmacshalgan contrasts with fourteen farming families in the Erris union. Although the population of Kilmacshalgan declined from 346 to 180 over the years 1901–1941, a reasonable sized population remained. The Erris parishes however had a population of only twenty two persons in 1941, having decreased from 236 in 1901 (91 per cent decrease.)

Table 2. Analysis of the populations of Kilmacshalgan parish and
Kilcommon Erris/Kilmore Erris union.

	Kilmacshalgan	Kilcommon Erris & Kilmore Erris
Population in 1901	346	236
Families in 1901	71	67
% farming households in 1901	80.28	20.90
% coastguard households in 1901	0.00	35.82
% born in Mayo, Sligo or Rosc.	86.99	39.41
Population in 1941	180	22
Families in 1941	49	10
% decrease in population	47.98	90.68
% decrease in families	30.99	85.07

Source: manuscript census returns in N.A.

In 1901, the Church of Ireland community in Counties Mayo and Sligo enjoyed a better standard of housing than their Roman Catholic counterparts.[11] 23.7 per cent of houses occupied by Church of Ireland persons were class 1 compared with 2.6 per cent in the total population. Only two class four houses in the entire diocese were populated by Protestants.[12]

A series of townlands were selected,[13] on the basis that they each contained at least two Church of Ireland farming families, the remainder of the population being Roman Catholic, with the exception of Ballysakeery parish, where some farming Presbyterians resided.[14] There were a total of 187 households in these townlands. Throughout the remainder of this chapter, this sample will be referred to as '187 households (or '187 farms' when farm size or valuation is studied.) The housing conditions of this sample were examined.[15] The expected findings are that more Church of Ireland houses were class two and fewer Church of Ireland houses were class three confirming that Church of Ireland persons resided in better houses. This is substantiated by the fact that the average Church of Ireland house had more rooms, more windows, and a higher percentage had permanent roofs. The degree of literacy among householders was, as expected, low in the Roman Catholic community and higher in the Church of Ireland and Presbyterian communities. It was unexpected to find that the average number of occupants in Roman Catholic households (3.77) was less than in Church of Ireland households (5.16) and less again than in Presbyterian households (6.63). It might be imagined that this was due to a larger number of servants in Protestant houses, but this is not borne out in the census returns, which show that Protestants (at the social level of small farmers) employed no more servants or live-in labourers than did Catholics.

A study of the nature of the outhouses on the chosen sample of 187 farms provided an opportunity to examine whether there was a difference in the nature of farming between the communities. As expected there was greater number of outhouses per house among Church of Ireland farmers, (4.46 Church of Ireland:2.48 Roman Catholic) indicating a greater level of prosperity and maybe reflecting the fact that they may have held leases of these farms for generations, whereas security of tenure for Catholics would have been comparatively recent. An analysis of the types of outhouses reveals that twice as many Protestants as Catholics owned a horse and a Protestant was ten times more likely to own a coach.[16] In every type of outhouse, the Protestant was better off, with the exception of dairies suggesting that Protestants owned more cattle, pigs, horses and were able to pursue a more profitable method of farming than their Roman Catholic neighbours.[17]

The Church of Ireland population of the area was unique in Ireland because it was composed mainly of small farmers. In a sample of seventy-two Church of Ireland farm holdings, (in 187 farms) for the year 1901, forty-three Church of Ireland farmers (63 per cent) held farms of under forty acres and of less than £20 valuation. Yet, as will be shown in the next chapter, it was this farming community that was the mainstay of the church in the region. They may not have been as poor as their Roman Catholic counterparts, but they were not rich.

By 1940, although the link with Britain was severed, the landed classes gone, the management of the country in Roman Catholic hands, many of these families remained. Throughout the period of the land war and the land acts there was considerable pressure on them to leave,[18] and yet every farm studied, passed in its entirety into Protestant ownership, and remained in Protestant hands until 1940. By combining the cancelled books in the Valuation Office with the census returns of 1901 and 1911, it was possible to analyse this ample of 187 farms on the basis of acreage, valuation of land, valuation of buildings, (valuation records) and religion of family. A total of 187 farms were studied, seventy-two Church of Ireland, 108 Roman Catholic and seven Presbyterian. The purpose of this section is to establish whether Church of Ireland farms were of similar size and valuation as neighbouring Roman Catholic farms. There are shortenings associated with this method, and it should be borne in mind that this is not necessarily a representative sample of the diocese.

There were few Roman Catholic farms larger than seventy acres in the sample and the majority of Roman Catholic farms were smaller than twenty five acres. It can also be seen that there was no discernible difference between Church of Ireland farms and Presbyterian farms. The Church of Ireland farms ranged in size from under ten acres to over 120 acres, the majority being between twenty-five and forty-nine acres. In contrast, the majority of Roman Catholic farms were in the ten to twenty-four acre range. Although this would suggest that Protestant farmers in the diocese were relatively comfortably off, there is some evidence of poverty among Protestants in the region.[19] In 1925

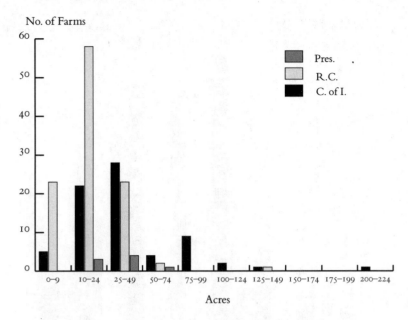

No. of Farms

Pres.
R.C.
C. of I.

Acres

6. Sizes of farms (acres) in sample of 187 farms.

three girls from Kilglass parish were sent to Sligo orphanage. They returned after a number of months. One died in 1934 aged about ten years. Their father was a farmer from Carrowhubbock. Also in Kilglass parish another girl of a farming background was sent to the female Orphan House in Dublin in 1935.

The years 1915–30 were crucial in the history of this region. The implementation of the land acts had an impact which was felt most in the counties of Connacht where land was compulsorily purchased and subdivided. Although some vendors maintained property in the area, not all resided in Mayo or Sligo and many left after the creation of the Irish Free State. The large farms of the Connacht counties were completely divided by 1930 whereas in other provinces this division occurred later. This decrease in the number of larger farms and departure of strong farmers, many of whom were members of the Church of Ireland, occurred in the very area of the country where Protestants were most sparse. Although the numbers of Church of Ireland farmers involved were reasonably small, the effect of the departure of many of the wealthier and the better educated in the community was devastating.

To provide a wider context of the pattern of Sligo Protestant landholding in 1926 the pattern of County Laois can be examined.[20] The following pattern of landholding emerged. The lower number of large farms (both Catholic and Protestant) in the western region became obvious. (figures 7 and 8) The average size of farms, both Catholic and Protestant, in County Sligo was significantly smaller than in County Laois. It is evident that Sligo Protestant

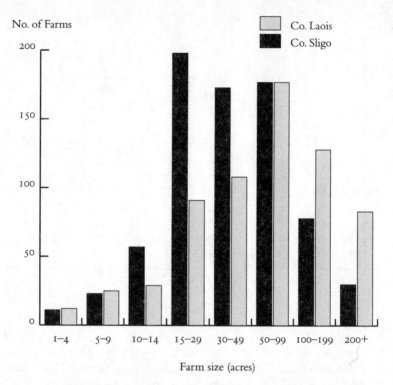

7. Church of Ireland farms, Counties Sligo and Laois, 1926 census.

farmers did not own large farms to the same degree as did Protestant farmers in the east of the country,[21] although their farms were larger than those of their Roman Catholic neighbours.

One reason often cited for the decline in the Church of Ireland Community is the pattern of marriage and fertility. The 1901 census demonstrates that, in terms of marriage and fertility, Protestants and Catholics behaved identically at the turn of the century. However, using data from the 1926, 1936, 1946 and 1961 censuses, it is clear that Protestant fertility declined drastically while Catholic fertility remained at the same high level as in 1901.[22] As regards fertility, Protestants throughout the twenty-six counties behaved in a similar fashion which was markedly different to the pattern of Catholic fertility.

The 1901 census shows that the percentage of females aged between twenty-five and thirty-five who were married was 42.86 for the Church of Ireland population of the diocese and 43.61 for County Sligo as a whole. This criterion is referred to as nuptiality. This confirms, as has often been claimed,[23] that in respect of marriage members of the Church of Ireland behaved in an almost identical fashion to their Roman Catholic counterparts at the end of the nineteenth century.

Nuptiality amongst Church of Ireland females and Roman Catholic females changed little after 1901. The situation with regard to fertility was totally different. The fertility rate remained high amongst Roman Catholic females (292 in 1946 compared to 310 in 1901) but fell amongst Church of Ireland females (175 in 1946 compared to 278 in 1901), caused not by a rise in the age of marriage but it would appear, by a conscious decision to limit the size of families. By 1946, the average age of first marriage of Church of Ireland females was thiry, and nuptiality of the Church of Ireland community was fifty five, implying that most females married, but at a late age.

In 1901 33.34 per cent of the combined total population of Counties Mayo and Sligo were under sixteen years of age and 34.45 per cent of the Church of Ireland population of the diocese was aged less than sixteen years (or 33.54 per cent when adjusted for the influence of the coastguards). This confirms that the Protestant birth rate equalled the Catholic birth rate in the fifteen years preceding 1901. However the average number of children born to couples married between 1916–1920 was 5.66 for Catholics and 3.29 for Protestants. This mirrors the findings of D.H. Akenson.[24]

This figure may not show the ultimate size of complete families. It is likely that after the census of 1961, additional children were born into marriages

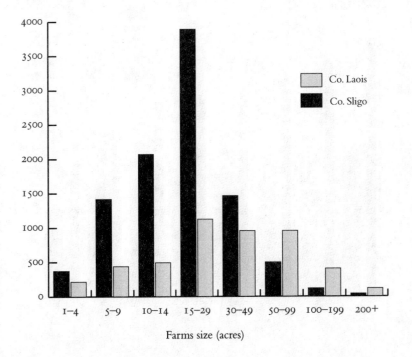

8. Roman Catholic farms, Counties Sligo and Laois, 1926 census.

especially those of less than ten years duration. It suggests however, that as the twentieth century progressed, Protestants, both in Connacht and nationally, had a significantly lower level of reproduction than Catholics and that in terms of reproduction, Connacht Protestants behaved in an almost identical fashion to national Protestants. The percentage of childless marriages in non-Catholic marriages, consistently higher than in Catholic marriages, was not due to a later age of marriage among Protestant females.[25] There was a greater incidence of childless marriages among Protestants at all age groups. There is no obvious reason for this feature. By 1926 the birth rate was lower than the death rate, resulting in a declining population, even before the effects of emigration were taken into account. Simply put, between 1926 and 1946, there were insufficient Protestant births to replace those persons who died. Not only did this result in a declining population, it also resulted in an ageing population. Even if no Protestant emigration had occurred this community was in decline.

Much has been written by demographers and sociologists concerning this divergence in fertility. The question remains largely unresolved but one unquestionable fact remains, that Protestants began to limit the size of their families in the early years of the twentieth century. Their increased level of

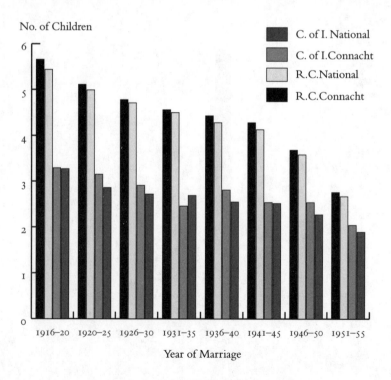

9. Average number of children per marriage.

education and increased literacy may have been relevant to their acquiring information about birth control, but I have been unable to find evidence of dissemination of this material at local level. There is the possibility that they abstained from any sexual activity once a certain number of children had been born. In either case they show themselves to have been a cohesive group, conforming to a changing set of social mores which were at variance from those of their parents and grandparents and from their neighbouring Catholics. Sligo Protestants, although they were a relatively isolated and self-contained community, became aware of and adopted the new reproductive patterns of Protestants in the early years of this century.

The second variable in population change is emigration.[26] The term 'emigration' should be more correctly read as 'migration or emigration' since this method of estimation is unable to differentiate between persons who left the county but remained in the Irish Free State and those persons who left the country. Bowen and Kennedy[27] both argue that emigration, not smaller families was the fundamental cause of the decline of the Protestant population of Ireland. Emigration post–1926 can be analysed, using data from the 1926, 1936, 1946 and 1961 censuses. The emigration of Church of Ireland persons 1911–1926 is difficult to estimate. Evidence of the boundary commission shows that fifty-five persons in seventeen families migrated to County Fermanagh. The coastguard population also left after 1922, in 1901 it had consisted of 257 persons in fifty-seven families.

Official census data for the years prior to 1926 do not give a breakdown by age and religion.[28] The census reports for the counties of Sligo, Laois and Kilkenny for the years 1926, 1936, 1946 and 1961 were studied.[29] County Laois was studied because it is roughly the same size as Sligo and contained approximately the same number of Protestants. It was possible that the establishment of Bord na Mona in Laois would influence the emigration patterns and thus Kilkenny was also studied, as a control county, but was omitted after scrutiny as there was no significant difference between Kilkenny and Laois.

It emerged that the pattern of emigration among Sligo Protestants post 1922 was closer to that of Sligo Catholics than to the nation-wide[30] norm for Protestants, that is emigration of single persons aged 15–25 and very little emigration of entire families.[31] In the two intercensal periods 1926–36 and 1936–46 there was very little emigration of entire families of Protestants from County Sligo but that between 1926 and 1936 twice as many Laois children migrated or emigrated compared to the national rate,[32] suggesting a social component resulting in the emigration of families from County Laois. It would appear that those younger Protestants and their families, who had remained in the County Sligo after the creation of the Irish Free State and who were present in the 1926 census, remained, at least until the 1946 census, but their offspring felt less inclined to remain or were obliged to emigrate at some stage after 1936.

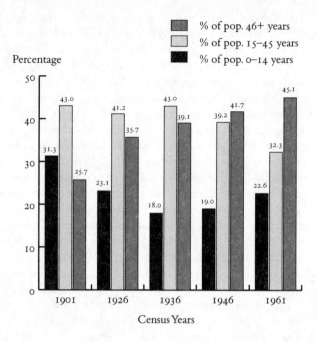

10. Percentage age distribution in County Sligo Church of Ireland population.

During the years 1926–46 the high level of emigration among young people from both religious communities was significantly above the national average for each group suggesting that the cause was regional economic depression. In the fifteen years after the Second World War Protestants and Catholics from Country Sligo emigrated to the same extent. In County Laois and nationally, the rate of emigration among Protestants was less than among Catholics. It could be said that in terms of emigration, during the years following the Second World War, the pattern of emigration of County Sligo Protestants was closer to that of County Sligo Catholics than it was to the national Protestant emigration trend. This high level of emigration suggests that although most farming Protestants may have remained on their farms after the creation of the Irish Free State, their children emigrated over the following decades.[33] Before the implementation of the land acts and the local authority acts and for as long as the landed estates continued to exist, there was sufficient local employment for second sons of Protestants. After 1922, positive discrimination in favour of Protestants had ended and emigration was essential for survival. Figure 10 shows an ageing population, which would in time lead to further decline.

When the decreased fertility was combined with the effects of emigration it resulted in an older population. In 1901 the average number of persons per household was 4.49, in 1941, it was 3.74 and in 1957 it was 3.04. Not only were there fewer Protestants in the diocese in 1941 than in 1901, a large number of those who remained were elderly parents whose offspring had already emigrated by 1941.

In summary, the majority of the Protestant population of Killala and Achonry diocese was located in County Sligo and a small section of County Mayo and the foundation for this pattern was determined in the seventeenth century. The population in areas outside this region (termed the plantation region) was largely transient and those who lived inside it were largely permanent, associated with agriculture and more likely to remain in the area after the creation of the Irish Free State. Although the Protestants of this area had better houses, larger farms and employed more prosperous farming methods, they were not as wealthy as Protestants in other areas of the country and instances of poverty existed. In terms of fertility Protestants and Catholics behaved identically at the turn of the century but in County Sligo Protestants began to limit the size of their families in the early years of the twentieth century, mirroring the national trend for Protestants. Widespread emigration of Sligo Protestants did not occur after the creation of the Irish Free State, (although almost all Protestants who were associated with the crown left in 1922), most Protestant farmers remained in the area in 1922 (although a significant number of farming Protestants did leave) and in subsequent decades the offspring of those who remained emigrated in greater proportions than did the offspring of Catholic farmers.

Church Finances

Prior to the disestablishement of the Church of Ireland, which occurred in 1870, small sparsely populated parishes had no concerns regarding their future. It was not the responsibility of the parishioners to provide an income for their clergy or to maintain church property. Although tithes *per se* had been abolished, the restructured method of incorporating tithe payments with rents guaranteed a steady income for the church, even in areas where there were few resident Protestants. The situation after disestablishment was different. Although the church had been well compensated for its loss of status and property, the onus fell on individual parishes to provide the funds for the maintenance of a parish infrastructure. These parishioners, especially tenant farmers, had no tradition of voluntary subscriptions to their church and in the early years after disestablishment the landed classes provided most of the necessary funding. Donations, generally of sums of £5 or greater, were given both by the landlords who were residents of a parish, and by those who owned land in the parish, although resident elsewhere. This pattern continued for the next twenty years, although as time went by, less well off parishioners began to donate some smaller sums of money.

Each parish had an 'assessment' imposed by the diocesan council. This assessment was determined primarily by the number of parishioners and amounted to the level of funding which the diocesan council considered the parish capable of generating. In those parishes where the contributions to the parish amounted to more than their assessments, the surplus was placed in the 'poor parishes fund'. This never happened in Killala and Achonry. When a parish was unable to meet its assessment it was subsidised by the poor parishes fund. At the diocesan synod of 1871, the first of an independent church, it was decided that no district should be maintained as an independent parish for which there was not a prospect of providing an income of £200 a year – except in exceptional cases. For the next ten years parishes struggled to meet their assessments and Kilcommon Erris (Belmullet), Killaraght (Gurteen), Kilmacteigue and Tubbercurry each received a grant of £500 towards their assessment funds, being as they were, 'almost destitute of resident gentlemen, members of the church'.[1] At the diocesan synod of 1879 it was noted that in the entire Mayo section of Achonry, where 170 church members lived, only five subscriptions from residents had been received, almost half of the 1,400 families in the diocese had given nothing at all. Rev. John Constable of Swinford (Kilconduff) wrote to all the absentee landlords of his parish. One reply stated 'I can't help you in Kilconduff. If the government have taken your property, so much the worse, but I don't think it is my duty to keep the church open there.' Another clergyman made reference to a nobleman, probably Viscount Dillon, who drew £26,000 per annum out of Ireland and did not subscribe, except a paltry sum to Castlerea. During the 1880s, however, the synod of Killala and Achonry diocese, in common with all other synods, reported a healthy improvement in finances. However, over the next thirty years successive land acts diminished the value of the property of the landed classes and agrarian unrest undermined morale. In spite of the fact that individual parishes were beginning to become self-reliant, the church had another cause for concern. In 1870, it had invested 50 per cent of the money it had received at disestablishment in the form of mortgages on landed estates. When the land war caused a dramatic fall in land values, this investment was largely worthless. In addition to the landed classes providing much of the day to day income of the church at parish level, they also had borrowed a large proportion of its reserve capital. By 1886, the Representative Body of the Church of Ireland was extremely aware of the financial difficulties, when the future of the large estates became uncertain.

In 1894 the *Irish Ecclesiastical Gazette* explained the danger of the situation by saying that the landlords would be left with sufficient income to maintain themselves and their families, but could no longer be expected to take responsibility for the welfare of the church or their former tenants.[2] It was impressed on the vestries that unless parochial assessments were met, entailing increased subscriptions from parishioners not associated with the landed, amalgamation of parishes and closure of churches was inevitable.[3]

The reality of the situation is clearly shown in the wording of the following notice, which suggests that a clergyman in the parish of Castleconnor should not have to rely on the parish for his income.

> I know of no more delightful, quiet parish in which to end the evening of a life than Castleconnor or Killanley, along the Moy, four miles from the railway at Ballina. The loving influence of the Dean made the parish like one family. The income of Castleconnor is only £150 p.a. There is a glebe house and thirty-two acres of land at a rent of £5. It is eminently suitable for an elderly clergyman of private means.[4]

At the synod of 1920, the dire state of clerical incomes was outlined. The only remedy was the large scale compulsory union of parishes. A special general synod was convened for the following November for this purpose, the result of which was the Minimum Stipend Act. The act set out a minimum stipend for future incumbents of £400 a year with a free residence and a minimum stipend of £200 a year for curates. Following the adoption of these guidelines by the Killala and Achonry diocese, all parishes except for Ballina (Kilmoremoy) and

Crossmolina were forced to amalgamate. The former had a sufficient middle income parishioner base, the latter was mainly maintained by the Pratt family. The biggest obstacle to amalgamation was distance. In 1920, Rev. Charles McQuaide told of a parish which even before amalgamation had a rectory seven miles from the church, and a coastguard station eighteen miles away, where service was also held once a week, necessitating an overnight stay. The parish in question was probably the neighbouring parish of Kilcommon Erris (Belmullet).[5]

Every parish of the diocese saw their subscriptions fall as their benefactors, the landed classes, departed. Only where there existed a sufficient body of parishioners, capable of subscribing sufficient funds to maintain a parish, was the church capable of maintaining a presence. As space does not permit an analysis of the finances of each parish, the donations to the parishes of Kilmacshalgan and Killaraght will be examined.[6] The donations to Kilmacshalgan (Dromore West) parish are typical of those received by a parish which was viable without the help of large donations.[7] In contrast, Killaraght (Gurteen) parish was unable to subsist, being reliant of landlord contributions and having a much smaller number of Protestant households. The total donation of £9.16s. 0d. in 1941 was insufficient to justify the parish of Killaraght, it merged with Emlyfad in 1929.

Tables 3 and 4 show that the level of subscriptions in Killaraght fell from £50 in 1873 to £10 in 1941. Over the same period the number of subscribing parishioners decreased from twenty to eight. In Kilmacshalgan the number of subscribing parishioners more than doubled over the same seventy years, from twenty-eight in 1871 to fifty-nine in 1941 and over the same time range the level of donations also grew from £52 to £82. A closer look at the subscriptions to Killaraght reveals that from 1883 to 1912 most of the subscriptions were or £5 or more, whereas in Kilmacshalgan over the same period more

Table 3. Summary of donations for Killaraght Parish, 1873–1941.

	1873	1883	1893	1903	1912	1920	1931	1941
Total subscriptions (£)	50	50	37	31	37	27	14	10
Subscriptions less than £1 (£)	29	11	4	3	12	2	5	6
Subscriptions between £1 and £5 (£)	14	6	1	2	5	25	9	4
Subscriptions over £5 (£)	7	33	26	26	20	1	0	0

Reports to the Diocesan Synod 1873–1941
In R.C.B.L. and diocesan library

Table 4. Summary of donations for Kilmacshalgan Parish, 1873–1941.

	1873	1883	1893	1903	1912	1920	1931	1941
Total subscriptions (£)	52	140	78	84	70	99	96	82
Subscriptions less than £1 (£)	18	31	6	24	22	15	30	36
Subscriptions between £1 and £5 (£)	13	34	27	24	24	55	46	31
Subscriptions over £5 (£)	21	85	35	36	24	29	20	15

Reports to the Diocesan Synod
In R.C.B.L. and diocesan library.

than half of the monies received by the parish was given in sums of less than £5. This large number of small donations is typical of those received by parishes with many middle income parishioners, (landlord contributions were generally over £5). A listing of the subscribers to Killaraght shows that in 1901 Col. King Harman, Rockingham (landlord) gave £10, Col. Cooper, Markree (landlord) gave £12 and R. A. Duke, Newpark (landlord) gave £8. Out of a total of £37 only £7 was donated by resident parishioners. In contrast, in 1903 fifty-five less well off parishioners of Kilmacshalgan donated £48. If this subject of donations from small and middle-income donors is examined over the remaining years of the study it can be seen that the finds from small and medium donations in Kilmacshalgan continued to grow, whereas in Killaraght there was no increase in donations from this group.

In some parishes, the departure of the landed classes and the public servants entailed the departure of almost the entire body of parishioners. In 1883, the entire income of Kilconduff (Swinford) was donated by three persons.[8] When Kilconduff merged with Straide (Foxford) in 1926, Swinford church was closed and demolished. Aside from annual subscriptions, landlords could be relied upon to help maintain church buildings. In 1893, Kilconduff parish received £100 from Hugh C. Brabazon, 'for the purpose of keeping the fabric of the churches at Kilconduff and Killedan in good repair'.[9] After the demise of the estates, this responsibility rested entirely on the parish.

In the early years following disestablishment, Killoran parish was maintained by the O'Haras of Annaghmore House and the Percivals of Templehouse. After the land acts, the O'Haras remained in the parish and continued to donate £50–£55 per annum to Killoran parish until and beyond the end of the period of study. Alexander Percival gave £30 per annum until 1930 and established a trust which donated £18 per annum thereafter. This support was also augmented by the large number of small and medium contributors. The presence of fifty families, who gave small and medium sized donations, coupled with the continued support from the O'Haras and the Percivals ensured the continuance of Killoran parish.

Two other parishes were maintained by landed families who remained in the diocese, Crossmolina by the Pratt family of Enniscoe House and Ballysadare by the Coopers of Markree Castle.[10] Crossmolina parish did not follow the diocesan trend. Although most of the landed families left the parish and ceased to contribute to its upkeep, the Pratt family of Enniscoe House made up the shortfall in funds. A study of the donations however shows that the donations of the earl of Arran (£10), W. Featherstone-Haugh (£15), R. W. Orme (£15), Capt. W. Orme (£5), Thos. Rothwell (£5), G.H. Knox (£10), J.H. Knox (£5), ? Knox (£6), are replaced by a significant donation of £125.7s.5d. from J. Pratt of Enniscoe House. There was a trend of a cessation of subscriptions from the landed classes and the compensation by the increased donation of the Pratt family. The pattern suggests, however, that there was no onus on the middle and small donors to support the parish. Subscriptions from small donors (less than £1) fell from £41 in 1873 to £25 in 1941. The subscriptions of the middle donors stayed relatively constant: £32 in 1873 and £31 in 1941. Throughout the diocese, in every other parish which survived, the middle and small donation groups were the parishioners that ensured the continuance of the parish, here the Pratt family ensured its survival.

We now turn to the question of diocesan finances. With no parish producing a surplus, the finances of the diocese had to be very closely regulated. Over the seventy years of the study, the increased funds from small and medium sized donors compensated in part for the decrease in large donations. The number of contributors rose by almost three hundred persons, from 573 in 1873 to 861 in 1941, over a period when the population of the diocese actually dropped from 7,767 to 2,303, suggesting that the diocese was maintained in earlier years by a very small number of large donations and in later years by a much larger number of smaller donations. In 1873 one person in fourteen subscribed to the church, by 1941 this had risen to one person in three.

When disestablishment removed state support for the church, it was most acutely felt in sparsely populated rural parishes. The majority of parishes in the diocese could not meet the assessments levied on them by the diocesan synod and relied to varying degrees on diocesan support especially 'poor parishes grants'. During the years 1870 to 1900 Killedan (Kiltamagh) merged with Kilconduff, Dunfeeney (Ballycastle) with Lackan, and Castlemore (Ballaghaderreen) with Killaraght. The land war and the withdrawal of support from some of the landed classes[11] exacerbated the precarious parish finances and the creation of the Irish Free State removed further sources of funding. When this was combined with the loss of church capital invested in land, the result was compulsory amalgamation. The following resolution was passed at the 1917 diocesan synod before the creation of the Irish Free State:

> that a parish which has to depend to any considerable extent on diocesan and other grants to maintain its existence as a separate parish should cease to be so maintained if it is in the interests of efficiency to unite it to another.

The diocesan synod of 1917 recommended the amalgamation of the following parishes, Straid (Foxford), Kilconduff and Killedan; Kilglass and Castleconnor; Killala and Dunfeeney; Kilcommon Erris, Kilmore Erris and Poulathomas; Tubbercurry and Kilmacteigue. This marked the beginning of the comprehensive rationalisation of the church. In most areas it was necessary to amalgamate adjoining parishes. These amalgamations were enforced on the occasion of the death of the first clergyman in the parishes concerned as in 1926 when Rev. Arthur Manning of Killaraght died and the parish was united with Emlyfad and when in the same year Rev. Glenn of Skreen died and the parish was united with Dromard. In all cases of amalgamation church services in the parishes concerned were curtailed. There was frequently local opposition to amalgamation, but in some cases it was difficult to justify the maintenance of a church. (The maximum attendance in service in Killaraght at the time of amalgamation was sixteen).[12] The amalgamations of the diocese are shown in table 5 and figure 11.

Figure 11 shows that only two churches (Lacken and Curroy C.E. in Kilmoremoy parish) closed inside the plantation region whereas eight churches outside the plantation region were closed over the seventy years.[13]

In the earlier years of the study, parishes in the diocese frequently solicited donations from elsewhere in the country for funds to provide for scripture readers and for renovations to their churches, such as the advertisements placed in the *Irish Ecclesiastical Gazette* (see Appendix 2.)[14] This attitude that the Church of Ireland population in the rest of the county would come to their rescue continued until the 1940s. It was probably fostered by the donation of monies to sparsely populated parishes in the south and west of Ireland from the 'poor parishes fund.' The parish churches in Gurteen (Killaraght) and Ballymote (Emlyfad) were the focus of an appeal as late as 1929 when funds were collected to extensively renovate both churches. The parishes of the diocese appear to have been slow to develop a sense of self-reliance and only reluctantly assumed responsibility for their own affairs. This was probably due to their having no history of voluntary subscription prior to disestablishment and to the subsequent departure of their wealthier parishioners before the parishes had become fully established as independent units.

In conclusion, the parish structure inherited by the newly disestablished church in 1870 was not viable. Prior to 1870 the church was supported by

Table 5. The amalgamations of the diocese of Killala and Achonry.

Parish	Location of Church	Outcome of parish
Achonry	Achonry	merged with Killoran 1927, cathedral closed and deconsecrated in January 1998
Ballysakeery	Mullafarry	merged with Killala 1932, church closed 1975
Ballysadare	Collooney and Ballysadare	merged with Ballysadare C.E. 1927, both churches in use (1998)
Castleconnor	Castleconnor	merged with Kilglass 1931, with Kilmoremoy 1941, church in use (1998)
Castlemore	Ballaghaderreen	merged with Killaraght 1889, church closed and demolished 1926
Crossmolina	Crossmolina	merged with Dunfeeney 1933, church in use (1998)
Dromard	Beltra	merged with Skreen 1927, church in use (1998)
Dunfeeney	Ballycastle	merged with Lacken 1881, with Killala 19258, with Ballysakeery 1929, with Crossmolina 1933, church in use (1998)
Easky	Easky	merged with Kilglass 1941, church in use (1998)
Emlyfad	Ballymote	merged with Killaraght 1927, church in use (1998)
Kilcommon	Belmullet	merged with Poulathomas 1907, with Bangor 1914, Erris with Kilmore Erris 1926, with Crossmolina 1945, church closed 1968.
Kilconduff	Swinford	merged with Killedan before 1870, with Straide 1926, church demolished 1926.

Parish	Location of Church	Outcome of parish
Killedan	Kiltamagh	merged with Straide 1926, church closed and unroofed.
Killala	Killala	merged with Dunfeeney 1925, with Ballysakeery 1933, church in use (1998)
Kilglass	Kilglass	merged with Castleconnor 1931, with Easky 1941, with Kilmoremoy 1976, church in use (1998)
Killaraght	Gurteen	merged with Castlemore 1889, with Emlyfad 1927, church closed and unroofed 1967.
Killoran	Coolaney	merged with Achonry 1927, church in use (1998)
Kilmacshalgan	Dromore West	merged with Skreen 1949, church in use (1998)
Kilmacteigue	Kilmacteigue	merged with Tubbercurry 1925, church closed and unroofed 1979.
Kilmore Erris	Binghamstown	merged with Kilcommon Erris 1926, church closed and unroofed 1950
Kilmoremoy	Ballina	merged with Castleconnor 1941, with Kilglass 1976 church in use (1998)
Skreen	Skreen	merged with Dromard 1927, with Kilmacshalgan 1949 church in use (1998)
Straide	Foxford	merged with Kilconduff and Killedan 1926, with Kilmoremoy 1950, church in use (1998)
Tubbercurry	Tubbercurry	merged with Kilmacteigue 1925, with Achonry 1960, church in use (1998)

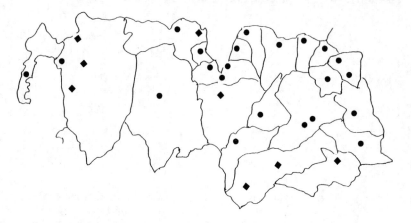

● Churches in use in 1940
◆ Churches closed between 1840 and 1940

11. Churches of the diocese, 1870–1940

tithes from the entire population collected through a charge on rents. Even without the land war the church could not have continued to function without some form of rationalisation. Following the merger of parishes, the resulting union frequently formed a viable unit, well capable of meeting its assessment. However there was only a need for a church in areas with a significant population. After the departure of the landed classes and the 'servants of the state' especially the coastguards, some of the coastal parishes had to re-evaluate their standing. Unpopular decisions were taken, parishes were merged and churches closed as the church moved from its position prior to 1870 where church finances were unrelated to the administration of parishes to the 1941 position that in the modern world every parish had to justify its existence.

Education

As well as reproducing itself physically and financially, the Church of Ireland community had also to pass on its social and cultural values. Most of this was normally done through the educational system. This section deals with the provision of education, initially under the control of the various bible societies and in latter years under the control of the national board of education. At the outset, the majority of schools under the control of the Church of Ireland were supported by bible societies, and as such were controlled from elsewhere. Alternatively they were controlled by the Church Education Society which placed them in the hands of the local clergyman. The funding of these schools began to decline in the last quarter of the nineteenth century when the second reformation was accepted to be a failure. As the national schools system developed, and after 1870 when the Church of Ireland agreed to take part, the control of schools came into the hands of the national board of education. Usually the local clergyman was manager and a local landowner acted as the patron.

When the national school system was proposed for Ireland in 1831, it was strongly resisted by all the main churches including the Roman Catholic church, the Church of Ireland, and the Presbyterian church. The Church of Ireland was afraid that they would not be in control of what was taught and that the scriptural teaching provided under the national education scheme was inadequate. Before 1831, schooling for Protestant children had been provided by the London Hibernian Society, the Irish Church Missions, the Island and Coast Society and the Kildare Place Society. The latter was in receipt of an annual parliamentary grant, the other societies were funded by the evangelical wing of the church, with most of the funds coming from England. To counter the effects of the national school system, the Church of Ireland established the Church Education Society for Ireland, which in due course took over the administration of the London Hibernian School Society and the Island and Coast Society. The purpose of these schools was two-fold, firstly to provide an educational environment where Protestant children would not fall under the influence of Roman Catholic or Presbyterian teachers and clergymen and secondly to educate, and also to some extent to indoctrinate Roman Catholic children in the ways of the Church of Ireland.

In the first half of the nineteenth century, there was little or no formal education in the west of Ireland. The arrival of the Church Education Society filled a void in some areas of the diocese, and while the education was decidedly directional in character, scripture being read daily at a time when this was not approved of by the Catholic hierarchy, at least it provided an education with definite standards and training for its teachers. Twenty-seven schools were subsidised by the Church Education Society in the 1850s but had ceased to function by 1860. Sixteen of these schools were located in the Erris region (Kilmore Erris parish and Kilcommon Erris parish). This region had one of the sparsest Protestant populations in the diocese, even in the 1860s. However it was the focus of intense proselytising activity during and after the Famine. Finances for these schools were withdrawn during the 1850s when the Church Education Society could no longer continue to fund schools in areas with few Protestants.

With the funding for the Kildare Place Society withdrawn,[1] the Church Education Society found it very difficult to maintain a schooling system and realised that it had to adapt to changing circumstances. In 1860, Archbishop Beresford, the primate, recommended to the general synod that they join the national school system. This about turn was a pragmatic decision. The second reformation had been generally accepted to have failed, and funds from England for the conversion of Roman Catholics were diminishing.[2] The future of parish schools was in doubt. The grant to the Kildare Place Society had ceased with the introduction of the national school system. From that date the church itself had to fund its schools. The decision to join the national school system, while terribly unpopular at the time, with hindsight was the only possible method of ensuring a denominational education for the sparse Protestant populations of the diocese. Those schools which could meet the criteria for entry to the national school system, applied to join. Of those that could not, some continued to be maintained by the Church Education Society, others were amalgamated to form viable schools which could become part of the national system, others were forced to close, some struggled along for up to fifty or sixty years before closing, and some were taken over by the Erasmus Smith Board. Parish clergyman were keen to ensure their schools were part of the national system. Parishes with 'weak' schools, which did not have sufficient numbers to join the national system, were subsidised by the Church Education Society.

There were stringent rules concerning teaching of religion in national schools. Crossmolina school was admonished for having bible texts on the walls that had been in situ when the school was run by the Church Education Society.[3] The national board of education stated that the texts could only be displayed during the times set for religious instruction. When a child attended a school that was under the control of a different denomination from that of his parents it was necessary for parents to sign a certificate agreeing to the circumstances.[4]

The formation of schools raises the question of their effectiveness. One way of measuring this is through the literacy of Church of Ireland persons in the diocese. In 1871, 1881 and 1891 the level of literacy amongst Church of Ireland persons, defined as the ability to write, was much higher than amongst Roman Catholic persons. In 1871 between 30 to 50 per cent of Catholics in the County Mayo section of the diocese were literate compared to an average of 80 per cent among Protestants. In the County Sligo section of the diocese literacy was higher among both communities, approximately 50 to 60 per cent among Catholics and 80 to 90 per cent among Protestants. This inter-county difference was maintained over the following decades, reflecting the poverty and inaccessibility of some of the County Mayo sections of the diocese. Kilmore Erris and Kilcommon Erris regions fared the worst, by 1891 they showed a level of illiteracy of 61 per cent and 69 per cent respectively, which was twice the average for the rest of County Mayo. Protestants in these parishes showed the same high level of literacy found elsewhere among Protestants, suggesting that the Church of Ireland persons in these parishes were a community apart and were not as materially or educationally impoverished as the Roman Catholic population.

Many clergymen noted in their return to the Sunday School Society, in 1881 and 1882, that levels of attendance in day schools were satisfactory.

> There are no Protestant children to be found in this neighbourhood who do not attend day school sufficiently to learn to read and write. Much of them learn much more. The only – being the poverty of – which obliges them to work and want of clothes. There has been no noteworthy changes in the last year in the circumstances of the school. The societies are most valuable in supplying Bible textbooks for the teachers.
>
> 7 Feb. 1883
>
> E.T. Hewson[5]

Table 6. Schools under the auspices of the C.E.S. in 1870, showing local funding and number of children on the roll.

Parish	School	£.	Roll	Parish	School	£.	Roll
Achonry	Tubbercurry	48	70	Emlyfad	Ballymote m.	30	34
Ballysadare	Collooney m.	45	50	Emlyfad	Ballymote f.	30	36
Ballysadare	Colloney f.	38	36	Kilglass	Valentine	36	18
Ballysadare	Collooney inf.	32	33	Killoran	Ardcree	30	103
Ballysadare	Ballysadare m.	43	40	Killoran	Coolaney	25	73
Ballysadare	Ballysadare f.	22	33	Killoran	Creevane	48	40
Ballysadare	Lugnadiffa	24	84	Killoran	Templehouse	46	96
Ballysadare	Stonehall	13	43	Killoran	Clara	89	
Castleconnor	Scurmore	65	23	Kilmacteigue	Kilmacteigue	16	24
Crosmolina	Moygounagh	29	28	Kilmacshalgan	Dunowla	30	84
Dromard	Dromard, Killala,	19	45	Skreen	Skreen m.& f.	65	70
Dromard	Dromard, Achonry	22	45	Skreen	Skreen training	178	73

(Table title row: "Schools under the auspices of the C.E.S. in 1870, showing local funding and number on roll"; column group headings "Local Funding")

Source: Report of the C.E.S., 1870, Ms. 154/7, in R.C.B.L.

The number of schools which were not under the national board decreased from thirty-six schools in 1871 to six in 1911. These schools relied entirely on local and church funds and frequently the local component was of a significant amount. Each year a collection was taken in most parish churches for the upkeep of the parish school. Most of the local funding came from the landed classes and not from the general body of parishioners. Appeals were frequently made for funds to help those schools with smaller numbers.[6] Most parishes with a viable school joined the national system. In many cases it was necessary to amalgamate male and female schools to meet the required number on the roll to join the national school system. To some extent this represented a relinquishing of control by the church in that standards of tuition were imposed and regulations regarding the teaching of religion had to be complied with.

As the numbers of children declined school attendances fell. The decrease in the number of Church of Ireland schoolchildren in Skreen parish is detailed in the preacher's book. The decline, fifty-two children in 1897 to sixteen children in 1929 (77 per cent decrease) is striking and could only be sustained by a parish which had a large population. When schools no longer met the criteria for inclusion in the national school system (usually owing to a fall in number of children on roll), they were struck off. After this occurred, some schools were again assisted by the Church Education Society, which by this time had meagre resources at its disposal. The Department of Education of the Irish Free State was sympathetic to the difficulties of the small, usually one-teacher Protestant schools. These schools were only struck off if the number of pupils on the rolls was lower than seven for two consecutive years. This generous treatment was not afforded to Catholic schools and was an acknowledgement of the problems of providing denominational education in sparsely populated areas.[7]

By 1900 only three schools remained under the auspices of the Church Education Society, Achonry, Kilmacteigue and Foxford (table 7). It became clear that these were not viable and they were forced to close; Achonry in 1903 and Kilmacteigue in 1910. In 1926 the Glen school (Ballinglen) in Dunfeeney was sold and the following year Gurraunard school (Crossmolina),[8] and Scurmore school (Castleconnor) were sold.[9] Foxford school closed in 1931. Dromard (Larkhill) was struck off from the national board in 1912 and the children transported to Lugnadiffa school. In Crossmolina the parish school had been forced to close in the spring of 1922, due to declining numbers. It reopened in 1931, with twenty-three children on the roll and a further twenty-one other children in the parish who were under school age. A further eight children resided in outlying districts, and could attend the school, if transport could be arranged.[10] By 1934, it was reported that there were seventy-five children of school-age and under in the Crossmolina parish, but that many of them lived far away from the school. Ballymote (Woodfield) fell out of the national system in 1930, owing to low numbers. It was helped for many years by the Church Education Society. It had eight children on the

Table 7. Church Education Society Schools, 1880–1930

Parish	School	1880	1881	1884	1885	1886	1888	1890	1900	1910	1920	1930	1940
	Schools under the auspices of the Church Education Society.												
Castleconnor	Scurmore	✓	Closed										
Castleconnor	Castleconnor	✓	Joined national system										
Kilglass	Leaffoney	✓	✓	✓	✓	✓	✓	✓	Joined national system				
Kilmacshalgan	Dunowla	✓	✓	✓	Closed								
Kilmoremoy	Curroy	✓	✓	✓	✓	✓	Closed						
Killoran	Coolaney	✓	✓	✓	✓	✓	✓	Closed					
Killoran	Clara	✓	✓	✓	Closed								
Killoran	Currane	✓	✓	✓	✓	✓	Closed						
Killoran	Ardaree	✓	✓	✓	Closed								
Killoran	Templehouse	✓	✓	✓	✓	✓	✓	Joined national system					
Achonry	Achonry	✓	✓	✓	✓	✓	✓	✓	✓	Closed 1903			
Emlyfad	Ballymote m.	✓	✓	✓	Unable to acertain but these schools were								
Emlyfad	Ballymote f.	✓	✓	✓	Maintained by C.E.S.after 1930								
Ballysadare	Lugnadiffa m.	✓	✓	✓	✓	✓	Joined national system						
Ballysadare	Lugnadiffa f.	✓	✓	✓	✓	Closed							
Ballysadare	Stonehall	✓	✓	✓	✓	✓	✓	| Joined national system					
Ballysadare	Ballysadare	✓	✓	✓	Joined national system								
Toomore	Foxford	✓	✓	✓	✓	✓	✓	✓	✓	✓	✓	✓	✓ Closed
Kilmacteigue	Kilmacteigue	✓	✓	✓	✓	✓	✓	Closed 1915					
Dunfeeney	Ballycastle	✓	✓	✓	✓	Taken over by Erasmus Smith Trust							
Easky	Killeenduff	✓	✓	✓	✓	Taken over by Erasmus Smith Trust							

Extracted from the Reports of the Church Education Society, for the years 1880–1950

roll in 1930, with an average attendance of six, by 1935 this had dropped to three on the roll. At the end of the period of study, the school was still open, ten Protestant children being transported in to maintain the numbers. The cost of transport was subsidised by the Church Education Society. By 1940 it was also subsidising the transport of children to Tubbercurry, Leyny, Easky and Lugnadiffa schools, (and Killala from 1945). In later years and to the present day, this has been the role of the Church Education Society.

Certain areas of the diocese were bereft of any Protestant schools, either church schools or national schools. Rev. Kingham in Swinford had a governess resident in his house in the 1901, as did many land-owning families. According to the 1901 census, thirty-two persons were involved in the provision of education; ten governesses and twenty-two teachers. No governess was native to the area; three had been born in England, four in the north of Ireland. There appears to have been a policy of not employing locals where the care of children was concerned.[11] Two-thirds of the teachers, (eight persons out of twenty-two) came from outside the diocese and almost all persons (twenty persons out of twenty-two) were under forty years of age. It is interesting to note that all married teachers were men, women may have had to resign on marriage. The national board had a ruling that a rural school of less than thirty-five pupils should be in the charge of a master, but that a mistress should be appointed to schools of smaller numbers.[12]

The diocese of Killala and Achonry did not possess a secondary school. There was a diocesan school for the united diocese of Tuam, Killala and Achonry in the town of Tuam in the south of the diocese. It closed about 1880. The town of Sligo, five miles outside the diocesan boundary, in the diocese of Kilmore, had a number of schools which were attended by the Protestant population of County Sligo.

A school was established in Skreen, County Sligo by Rev. Edward Nangle, who had formed the Protestant settlement, at Dugort on Achill Island in the 1840s, to educate some boys towards the entrance examination for the Kildare Place Training School and others towards the entrance examination for Primrose Grange School, Sligo. Rev. Greer, in his book, *The Windings of the Moy*,[13] gives a good account of life in this school. Several of the boys came from the orphanage and training school attached to the Achill mission. The boys boarded with families in the locality and attended school as dayboys. As a boy, Rev. Greer boarded with Mrs. James Boyd of Carranree from 1863 to 1865. The school had a high standard: in 1900, two boys from Skreen, W. T. Doyle and H. V. Coulter won scholarships from the Incorporated Society for the Promotion of Protestant Schools in Ireland. Girls were also educated in a female section of the Skreen school and were prepared for the entrance examination of the Incorporated Society School in Roscommon (Ranelagh School.) The education given in the Skreen school was free, but each student gave an undertaking to repay £10 to the institution, when they first took up an appointment, the sum to be repaid at the rate of ten per cent of salary.

Clergymen frequently augmented their income by tutoring boys for entrance to Trinity College. The position of Rev. Crolly in Easky in 1884, with 300 parishioners augmenting his income by finding time to tutor boys contrasts with Rev. Kingham in Swinford in 1901, who employed a governess for his own children although he only had fifty-seven parishioners. The following advertisement placed in the *Irish Ecclesiastical Gazette* of 14 January 1884, is typical of those placed by clergymen during this period:

Home Education (Seaside)

Rev. George Croly, M.A., Double Prizeman and Honourman, Trin. Col. Dub., receives a limited number of pupils to board and educate. As Mr. Croly takes only a few pupils, they have all the advantages of constant personal care. By his method of teaching boys acquire a taste for books, instead of what too frequently happens – a dislike. Fees moderate. Home comforts; careful training and teaching. Highest references to parents of present and past pupils, or to Rev. Wm. Stubbs, F.T.C.D.; or Rev. Wm. Skipton, Ballina.

The roll books of Mariners School, Kilglass, County Sligo reveals that secondary education was commonplace in certain families and that the children from this parish proceeded to secondary schools throughout the country.[14]

In the decades prior to 1870, the provision of education underwent a gradual change from schools operated and controlled by evangelising societies to those directly controlled by the Church Education Society. Over the period of study, much of the control of these schools passed from the church to the national board of education. The decision to transfer much of the management of the schools was made on economic grounds, the national board assuming responsibility for the renumeration of teachers and the maintenance of standards. The day to day running of the school remained in the hands of the local clergyman and manager, but by the early years of the twentieth century most of the schools of the diocese were part of a national system of education.

Integration and segregation

This chapter investigates the extent to which the Church of Ireland population of Killala and Achonry diocese mixed with their Catholic and Presbyterian neighbours and to what degree their opinions differed from those of their Catholic neighbours. Were they a community apart or were they integrated into the general community of the region? Did mixed marriages occur? How segregated were they in terms of education? Was there any accusation or evidence of proselytising? What were their attitudes to the land war, division of the estates, home rule, and partition?

It would appear that the attitudes of the clergy and the laity of the Church of Ireland towards their children attending schools under the control of clergymen of different faiths varied a good deal from parish to parish. There is no clear pattern and it is not possible to say whether religious tolerance grew or diminished over time. Some clergymen, like Rev. Lynn and Rev. Perdue of Ballysakeery and Rev. Walker of Emlyfad, were vehemently opposed to Church of Ireland children attending Roman Catholic or Presbyterian schools, others like Rev. McCormick of Ballysadare had no objections. In 1898 Rev. Perdue voiced his fears regarding the local Presbyterian school in a letter to the *Irish Ecclesiastical Gazette* of 15 April 1898

> The schools . . . have almost ceased to do mission work amongst Roman Catholics, as was their original intention, and confine their attention almost exclusively to Church children. Every one of these schools has a tendency to become a nucleus of Presbyterianism and to weaken the church.

In 1907, Rev. Walker of Ballymote[1] (Emlyfad) sent the following circular to his parishioners, warning them against sending their children to any schools, other than the parish school:

> It may be well now to remind parents of the large educational endowments that are available for children of our Church; but before either sex can get the benefits, a series of stringent questions must be answered by the clergyman of the parish in which the candidates reside, and any defection of yours personally, or on the part of your children, from the sound Scriptural doctrines held by our ancient Church, may render it impossible for him to give such written answers as are essential, in order that these benefits maybe secured.[2]

The dangers of an integrated education were frequently remarked upon in the *Church of Ireland Gazette*, where many saw inter-denominational education as a forerunner to mixed marriages and leakage from the Church:

> . . . The small number attending each school shows the schools are situated in districts where the Protestant population is small. The future of our Church in such districts depends on these schools being efficiently maintained . . . if our children are educated in Roman Catholic schools, the associations formed are a ready road in many cases for mixed marriages.[3]

Not all clergy held this attitude. In Kilmacshalgan (Dromore West) the Presbyterian schools attracted a large number of Church of Ireland pupils, although the parish had its own school at Dunowla. In 1907 there were twenty-seven Church of Ireland pupils out of a total of thirty-eight on the rolls of the Presbyterian school.[4] Some clergy of all denominations were reasonably tolerant. When Mariners school, Kilglass parish, was opened in 1898, with an average attendance of twenty children (all Church of Ireland) Rev. MacHale, the local Roman Catholic parish priest, made no objection to its application, although it resulted in the removal of fourteen children from Enniscrone national school (Roman Catholic)[5] and in 1900 when Leaffoney school was established the local Roman Catholic clergy made no objection, even though its existence resulted in three children being withdrawn from Quigabar national school and two children each from Rathlee Boys national school and Rathlee Girls national school.[6]

In 1904, Arthur Foster, the schoolmaster of Lugnadiffa school (Ballysadare parish) had his salary cut from £52 to £32 in 1906 after his Roman Catholic pupils began to attend a recently opened Catholic school 200 yards away (Lugawarry school).[7] He complained that the establishment of Church of Ireland national schools in Leyny, in the adjacent Killoran parish and Larkhill in the adjacent Dromard parish combined with the newly opened Catholic school in Lugawarry militated against him.[8] In 1906 the attendances at the four schools in were Leyny (18), Larkhill (21), Lugnadiffa (12) and Lugawarry (12, all Roman Catholic). At no time did he voice any resentment towards Roman Catholic children attending Roman Catholic schools, he merely resisted his salary being decreased by circumstances beyond his control. In 1920 Rev. McCormick of Ballysadare and Collooney advised against a van service which would ferry fifteen Church of Ireland children to the parish school in Collooney, these children had been attending a Roman Catholic school nearer their homes. At a time when his own school was under pressure of falling numbers, he stated that he had the utmost confidence and respect for the manager, Rev. Fr. Doyle and Mr. McGowan, principal of the Roman Catholic school.[9]

The correspondence regarding the opening of Lugawarry school, mentioned above, provides an insight into both sides of a contentious issue. The landlord, O'Hara of Annaghmore, had provided three schools in the early years of the nineteenth century, Leyny, Larkhill and Lugnadiffa. These were all under the control of the Church Education Society and the local Church of Ireland clergy and were staffed by Protestant teachers. When Rev. Connaughton was appointed Roman Catholic parish priest he set about establishing a school under Catholic management. Charles O'Hara refused to provide a site for the school and strenuously objected to its opening. He stated that there were sufficient schools in the area and that an additional school would diminish the numbers and quality of the existing schools. He offered that Rev. Connaughton or his curate could have the use of the school for thirty minutes per day to instruct the pupils in accordance with Roman Catholic church. Fr. Connaughton refused stating that he could not devote the time to educate the children and that this should be the duty of the school-teacher. Fr. Connaughton ordered the withdrawal of the Roman Catholic children from Lugnadiffa school and established a temporary school at Lugawarry which was recognised by the national board.[10] It is difficult to state whether Major O'Hara objected to the establishment of an additional school or the establishment of an additional Catholic school.

The *Sligo Champion* of 1904 gave details of some of the proselytising activities of Rev. Walker of Emlyfad. When a young girl names Moran, who was employed in the household of a minor landlord, Charles Phibbs,[11] began to attend Church of Ireland services, the local Roman Catholic community was enraged. The Roman Catholic bishop of Achonry, Dr. Lyster, referred to Mr. Phibbs as a proselytiser in correspondence to the National Board of Education.[12] Mr. Phibbs was threatened and boycotted, to the extent that a police hut was erected at his house, occupied by up to twenty policemen. The girl was moved out of the area, but the police presence remained. Mr. Phibb's actions were severely resented and no-one in the town, either Catholic or Protestant would supply him with labour or transport.[13] When Phibbs ran out of hay, the locals refused to carry for him, but he was assisted by Canon Walker and Canon Heather and by the L.O.L. 617.[14]

Charges of proselytism were relatively rare however. In general the communities lived side by side without animosity or undue distrust. When Rev. Crolly left Easky parish after twenty-five years the local nationalist newspaper commented on this departure as follows:

> The poor would miss him, the struggling classes would miss him for he anticipated their wants and promptly came to their assistance in their trials, their troubles and their difficulties for he was large hearted and generous.[15]

Both the Catholic Church and the Church of Ireland frowned on mixed marriages. The *Ne Temere* decree, which came into effect in 1908, was the cause of much strife. This decree stated that the children of all marriages, where one partner was Catholic, must in all circumstances be brought up in the Catholic faith. In Ireland, this was interpreted as giving the authority to Catholic parents and relatives to abduct the children, if necessary, and bring them up outside the home, as Catholics. Mixed marriages had always taken place. Before the passing of *Ne Temere*, it was not inevitable that the resulting family would be lost to the Protestant church. After its passing, the dominant position of the Catholic church was copper-fastened. Editorials in the *Church of Ireland Gazette* advised that the danger of mixed marriages should be avoided, and this was one reason why the attendance of Protestant children in schools under Roman Catholic control was to be discouraged. By 1923, the church realised it had a serious problem with diminishing numbers, noting:

> ... the leakage from the church occurs in the upper and middle classes, and that if anything we gain in the lower ... Whom are the daughters of our gentlemen farmers to marry? Not only have many of the men of their own station been killed in the war, but the young men of the same class are bound to get out of the country to find a living. We have not enough men to go round ... it is difficult for minorities to practice tolerance and survive.[16]

It urged active measures to cause the mingling of single Protestants. The new craze of dancing and dance halls was discouraged, since it was impossible to ensure that prospective partners would be Protestant. This attitude was similar to that of the Roman Catholic hierarchy. In their Lenten pastoral of 1924, they condemned ballroom dancing as 'the outcrop of the corruption of the age'.[17]

The attitude of Protestants to the Land League varied widely. The Land League itself embraced all persons whose views were in line with theirs. Mr. Timothy Sexton, M.P., said at a meeting in Ballymote:

> Let nobody say that there is any sectarian feeling in the movement. It is for the good of every man who suffers from landlord wrong, no matter what his creed may be, it is a movement against every landlord who is unjust, no matter if he pose as the most devout Catholic on earth.[18]

A second meeting was held to establish a branch of the Land League at Bricklieve, outside Ballymote. There were a good number of persons present, both Catholic and Protestant. Mr. McDermott and Mr. Cawley from the Ballymote branch attended and said that the same unity existed in Bricklieve as in Ballymote, where both Catholics and Protestants were members.[19] They added that the Catholic landlords of the south wanted to defeat the Land League and have their farms worked by labourers and that this plan had failed. The Protestant landlords of the north wanted to defeat the Land League and had said that its intention was to drive Protestants out of Ireland, but this was untrue and their plan had also failed.[20] The Land League did not have the support of the Protestant traders. When the Land League celebrated a victory over a land-grabber in Gurteen (Killaraght), bonfires were lit on every hill for miles around. In Ballymote a fife and drum band marched through the town, where all businesses were lit up, except for Protestant businesses.[21] Not all Protestant farmers supported the Land League. In 1880, the same year as the meetings in Ballymote and Bricklieve, a meeting of Orangemen was held in a house in Lugawarry outside Ballysadare.[22] It was suggested in the nationalist newspaper, the *Sligo Champion* that the landlord, Major O'Hara, was unduly lenient with tenants of this disposition who were in arrears with their rents.[23]

When the United League was formed in 1898 with the intention of redistributing land so that all farms could be of reasonable size, some Protestants were victimised. Cattle belonging to Protestant farmers were maimed in Dromard, Skreen and Easky. A Protestant house was burnt down in Dromore West, horses were injured in Ballymote and Ballysakeery, John Thompson, Ballysadare was boycotted and went bankrupt.[24] It would appear that these Protestant farmers were targeted not on the basis of their religion but because they held large farms and their treatment was no more severe than that meted out to Catholics with large farms. By the time that the division of the estates became a reality, both Protestant and Catholic tenant farmers engaged in negotiations. When a tenants committee was formed in 1904 to negotiate the purchase of the Hillas estate, Dromore West (Kilmacshalgan), a number of Church of Ireland tenant farmers were included: George Brett (Dunbeakin) and Robert Brett (Doonecoy), implying that they were approved of and were involved in the process of land purchase.[25]

The Protestant community held the Protestant Home Rule Association in utter contempt, describing its members as 'a bunch of men who attest their Protestantism by not attending church'[26] and in 1912 services were held in churches throughout the diocese against the threat of home rule. Nevertheless some Sligo Protestants supported the movement, albeit anonymously. When the Tenants Defence Organisation took up a collection in Ballysadare two contributions, one of 5s. 6d. and one of 1s. 0d. were received from persons both calling themselves 'Protestant Home Ruler'. It is important to note that these persons did not feel free to identify themselves.[27]

It is evident from the above examples that only tentative conclusions can be drawn regarding the attitudes of Protestant tenant farmers and events occurring nationally from 1880–1910. Some Protestants shared the aims of the Land League, the United Irish League and the home rule movement (albeit sometimes silently) while others opposed all change, preferring to maintain the landlord system and the link with Britain. There were probably many persons whose views fell somewhere between these two extremes. While the hierarchy of the Church of Ireland generally fell into the latter group, it would appear that many smaller tenants silently supported the reform movements. During the land war the Protestant tenant farmer was in a very difficult position. On one hand his clergyman and his landlord were demanding that he pay his rent, on the other hand he was vigilantly watched by the Land League, lest he disobey their dictats.

In summary it can be said that no firm conclusion can be drawn regarding the integration of the Church of Ireland, and Roman Catholic communities. On occasions and in some locations tolerance and co-operation existed while in others distrust and suspicion prevailed. There did not seem to be a geographic pattern or an evolution of attitudes over time, but it can be deduced that the presence of an ultra-Protestant or ultra-Catholic clergyman or a landlord who openly gave preferential treatment to members of one community was a hindrance to good inter-community relations.

Conclusion

The primary objective of this study was to discover why some areas in the diocese had large Church of Ireland populations while others had very small numbers of Protestants and to determine why some parishes with apparently large Protestant populations dwindled away while other parishes remained in existence. On examination of population trends and the financial pattern of the parishes in the diocese, it is evident that the two following factors were necessary for the continuance of a Church of Ireland population in a parish. The first factor related to land ownership, as determined in the seventeenth century. The second related to the parish situation at disestablishment, but this situation was determined primarily by the disposition of the landlord, both in 1870 and in the preceding two hundred years. The following criteria have emerged as essential for the continuance of a Protestant community. It was necessary for the landlord to be a committed Protestant, possibly one who imported a working class Protestant population, for whatever reason, either political or economic. It was beneficial that landlords be resident. It was also necessary that there existed at disestablishment, a sizable number of Church of Ireland persons, who needed to be middle income parishioners with the ability to contribute sufficient monies to maintain a parish, the people had to be bound to the area, either by their occupations, or by ownership of land or business and not transient parishioners, such as coastguards, employees in 'big houses', etc., and who were historically Protestant, not recently converted from Catholicism as a result of missionary activities.

A study of the population trends of the diocese reveals that emigration was the principal cause of population decline in the years after 1922. It would appear that this occurred more for economic than for social reasons. This high level of emigration is a manifestation of the lack of employment facilities for second sons (both Catholic and Protestant). The effect of an exodus of young adults of such a scale on an already sparse community, occurring incessantly over the decades, resulted in a diminished pool of prospective marriage partners. This had two consequences, firstly a lower or later rate of marriage and secondly a growing prevalence of mixed marriages, where the offspring were generally brought up outside the Church of Ireland. This study has established that in terms of emigration, Protestants in the west of Ireland behaved in a broadly similar pattern to Catholics but that in terms of marriage and fertility, these Protestants behaved like the national Protestant norm and quite differently to neighbouring Catholics.

The review of houses and outhouses and farms size belonging to the Church of Ireland population revealed the following facts: Church of Ireland farms were consistently larger and of greater valuation than Catholic farms and than the county and poor law union average and employed a more profitable method of farming than Catholic farmers. Church of Ireland housing conditions were consistently better than their Catholic neighbours. The Church of Ireland farms studied had been in Protestant ownership for many years and Church of Ireland farmers became the owner occupiers of their properties when the land acts were implemented. Notwithstanding the above comments, it must be repeatedly stated that most of the Church of Ireland farmers on the Killala/Achonry diocese, initially tenants and later owner-occupiers, were not large farmers. They may not have numbered among the extremely poor, but they were comfortable rather than rich. The contrast between the sizes of Protestant farms in Counties Laois and Sligo in 1926 illustrates this point. Whatever wealthy Protestants resided in this region were of the landlord class,[1] or were involved in industry.

It is evident from the financial study of the diocese, that there was only a viable future for the church in parishes where, by the turn of the century, contributions from the less well off parishioners formed a substantial portion of total monies received. The departure of benefactors, in the form of landed gentry, occurring so soon after disestablishment, forced each parish to justify its existence. The presence of a body of middle income parishioners was vital for the maintenance of a parish, and as explained in the first chapter, the existence or non-existence of this body of persons was determined prior to the Disestablishment of the church. By 1889, the *Irish Ecclesiastical Gazette* remarked that one-sixth of the diocesan funds came from charitable societies, such as the Hibernian Society, two-sixths came from absentee landlords, and three-sixths or half of the funds required to maintain the diocese were donated by resident church people, implying that the church could not be self-supporting and could not possibly maintain the number of churches and clergymen without substantial help from outside the diocese.[2] The decline in population and in diocesan funding resulted in a decrease in unions in the diocese from twenty-two in 1870 to twelve in 1940. It should be noted that the first series of amalgamations were proposed in 1917,[3] before the departure of the most of the landed classes and the creation of the Irish Free State. Irrespective of the land war and the creation of the Irish Free State, most of the parishes were never viable as individual parishes; amalgamations were inevitable and were hastened but not caused by the land war and the events of 1922.

Over the seventy years in question (1871–1940) most of the Church of Ireland schools in the diocese came under the control of the national board. Prior to 1870, the emphasis had changed from missionary schools intent on educating Catholic children (scripturally as well as academically) to providing Church of Ireland schools for Church of Ireland children. The criteria required

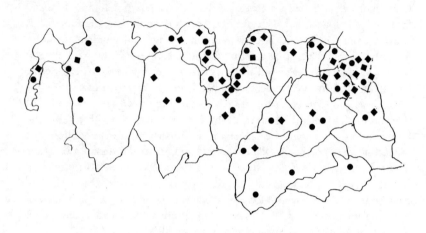

12. The diocese in 1871   ● Church   ◆ School

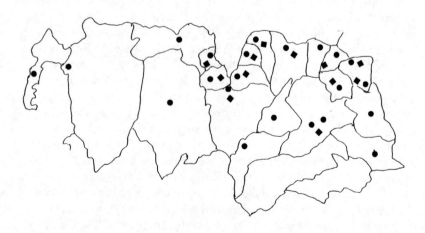

13. The diocese in 1940   ● Church   ◆ School

by the national board of education necessitated the amalgamation of smaller schools and the closure of others. The stringent conditions imposed by the national board regarding religious education of children of other denominations were complied with but sometimes only after inspections by the board.

This rationalisation of the Church of Ireland reflects the areas in which the Protestant population persisted. At the beginning of the period of study there were twenty-two unions with thirty churches and twenty-seven schools in operation. In 1940 there were twelve unions with twenty-three churches and fifteen schools. There was a definite need for Protestant churches and schools in some areas while in other areas there were few Protestants by 1940.[4] Sixty-six persons scattered throughout such a large area as the region outside the plantation zone could not be called a community whereas 2,442 persons concentrated in one portion of the diocese, the region inside the plantation zone, formed a stable and cohesive community.[5] To some extent population data and the above facts regarding the number of churches mask an ageing population and the evolving pattern of consolidation into County Sligo and Tyrawley region of County Mayo which becomes evident when the current (1999) situation is viewed.

The purpose of this study was to establish why the Church of Ireland died out in certain areas and survived in others, with reference to the influence of the land acts, the creation of the Irish Free State, emigration and education. It can be concluded that the foundation of the population patterns of the Church of Ireland population of the Killala and Achonry diocese were determined in the seventeenth century and that the inclusion or exclusion of a parish from the plantation region was the most important determinant of its outcome.

Appendix 1

Number of Church of Ireland heads of household giving their occupation as farmer in 1901. (Parishes marked with an asterix are outside the Cromwellian region)

Number of Church of Ireland Heads of households giving their occupation as farmer in 1901.							
	Households					Households	
Parish	Total	Farmer	Per cent	Parish	Total	Farmer	Per cent
Achonry	82	59	71.95	Kilconduff★	110	3	30.00
Ballysadare	100	58	58.00	Killala2	8	3	10.71
Ballysakeery	48	39	82.15	Killaraght	22	18	81.82
Castleconnor	40	27	67.50	Killoran	69	45	65.22
Castlemore★	12	4	33.33	Kilmacshalgan	71	57	80.28
Crossmolina	67	46	68.66	Kilmacteigue	12	9	75.00
Dromard	16	10	62.50	Kilmore Erris★	28	4	14.29
Dunfeeney	35	13	37.14	Kilmoremoy	100	23	23.00
Easky	54	32	59.26	Skreen		50	39	78.00
Emlyfad	63	32	50.79	Straide★	22	12	54.55
Kilcommon Erris	39	10	25.64				
Inside plantation region	930	539	57.96				
Outside plantation region	111	34	30.36				

Source: 1901 census returns, National Archives.

Appendix 2

The following appeal for funds was typical of those placed in the *Irish Ecclesiastical Gazette* and the *Church of Ireland Gazette*. This appeal was made in the *Church of Ireland Gazette* of 25 August 1905.

Union of Doonfeeney and Lacken
Diocese of Killala

APPEAL

The parishioners of this Union appeal earnestly for funds to enable them to repair and restore the Parish Church of the ancient Parish of Lacken, which is in a very dilapidated condition and in danger of falling into ruin.

Our total population, though somewhat over two hundred, is scattered over so wide an area – the Union being some twenty five miles long and on a an average eight miles broad – that it is absolutely necessary to maintain more than one place of worship.

Lacken Church is six miles from Ballycastle and is situated on the other side of a range of hills. Most of those who attend that church reside at an even greater distance from Ballycastle. Since 1900, when we issued our former appeal, we have thoroughly restores two of our churches, viz. the Parish Church, Ballycastle, and the Church of Ballinglin.

Of the £130 collected since 1900 for restoration, we received £50 from the Beresford fund and about £30 from resident parishioners.

Having no rich people amongst our permanent residents, and most of our church people being very poor indeed, we are obliged to appeal fors help to our brethren who are more fortunately circumstanced.

Although a debt of £20 still remains unpaid, we feel that we cannot put off any longer the work of restoring Lacken church, though it will cost about £40 to do what is absolutely necessary.

If those who are interested in the welfare of the Church in the poor and remote parts of the country will enable us to carry out this work, the Parishioners will undertake to pay off the small debt which is due from their own resources with as little delay as possible.

Subscriptions will be thankfully received by

W. J. Foley,
The Rectory, Ballycastle, Mayo.

The Lord Bishop of Tuam writes:-
This work is a necessity, it is not at all decorative but for the preservation of the fabric and decent fittings: and I fully approve this appeal.

Signed,   J. Tuam.

Received Lord Bishop of Tuam	£5 0 0
J.E. McCormick, Esq., J.P.	£5 0 0

Notes

INTRODUCTION

1 *C. of I.G.*, 5 October 1923.

2 *C. of I.G.*, 12 October 1923.

3 Jack White, *Minority report, The anatomy of a southern Irish Protestant,* (Dublin 1975) pp 61, 62, 65.

4 R.F. Foster, (ed.), *The Oxford illustrated history of Ireland,* (Oxford, 1989) p. 252.

5 J.J. Lee, *Ireland 1912–1985,* (Cambridge, 1989) p. 162.

6 *C. of I.G.*, 26 October 1906.

7 *C. of I.G.*, 29 December 1911.

8 The exception to this was the election of Bryan Cooper to the dáil.

9 Victor Griffin, *Mark of protest* (Dublin, 1993) p. 27.

10 For example, at a vestry meeting in Ballymote (Emlyfad) sympathy was extended by the parish to Mr. Graham for 'the shocking treatment which he was still receiving at the hands of lawless neighbours,' Minutes of the Select vestry, 12 October 1922, in R.C.B.L., MSS. P202/3/6.

11 *C. of I.G.*, 6 January 1922.

12 *C. of I.G.*, 5 February 1926.

13 *C. of I.G.*, 24 December 1930.

14 Quoted in Lee, *Ireland*, p. 167.

15 *C. of I.G.*, 5 December 1930.

16 The *Catholic Bulletin*, xxi, no. 3., March 1931, p. 210–211.

17 Lee, *Ireland*, pp 161–167.

18 Miriam Moffitt, 'The Church of Ireland diocese of Killala and Achonry 1870–1940,' Unpublished M.A. Thesis, N.U.I. Maynooth 1998, Appendix I, Electoral Results, Mayo and Sligo, 1800–1943.

19 The following nationalist newspapers were published weekly in the region, *Sligo Champion* (Sligo, 1836–current), *Western People* (Ballina, 1883–current), *Tyrawley Herald* (Ballina, 1844–1870),

Mayo Examiner (Castlebar, 1868–1903), *Connacht Telegraph*, (Castlebar 1828–current).

20 This support was given in 1886, on the condition that the home rule movement support denominational education.

THE CHURCH OF IRELAND COMMUNITY

1 Conversation with Mairéad Ni Murchadha, December 1997.

2 The Church of Ireland population of Ballysadare was 838 in 1871, whereas there were only 70 Church of Ireland persons in Kilconduff in the same year.

3 J.G. Simms, 'County Sligo in the eighteenth century,' in *J.R.S.A.I.* xci (1961), p. 153, Samuel Lewis, *A topographical dictionary of Ireland* (2 vols, London, 1837), ii, p. 566.

4 Arthur Young, *A tour in Ireland*, (1780), pp 223–43.

5 On Lord Shelbourne's estate.

6 *Speech of Rev. Michael Seymour,* quoted in T. O'Rorke, *History, antiquities and present state of the parishes of Ballysadare and Kilvarnet, in the county of Sligo,* (Dublin, 1878) p. 167.

7 Desmond Bowen, *Souperism: myth or reality* (Cork, 1970) pp 201–209, Liam Kennedy et al., 'The long retreat, Protestants, economy and society, 1660–1926,' in R. Gillespie and G. Moran (eds), *Longford, essays in county history,* (Dublin, 1991) pp 30–61.

8 In 1774, Thomas Fitzmaurice introduced northern weavers to Ballymote. He provided each with a slate and stone cottage cottages at the cost of £50 per weaver. James C. MacDonagh, *Ballymote and the parish of Emlyfad,* (Dublin, 1936) p. 119.

9 R.C.B.L, MS. P203/5.

10 In 1898 ten boys out of a total of fifteen boys in Mariners School, Kilglass were from coastguard families (Roll book of Mariners School, Kilglass, County Sligo in NA.).

11 This is based on the assumption that the majority of the persons in the Counties Mayo and Sligo, who were not members of the Church of Ireland, were Roman Catholics.

12 In Kilmorgan parish, Emlyfad Union, John McCormick, (73) an army pensioner and a widower, lived on his own in a class four house. In Farrangarode townland,

Castleconnor parish, Maria Cleary (59) and her nephew Robert Stenson (22), neither married, both agricultural labourers, lived in a class four house.

13 Lugbaun townland, Dromard Parish, Dunowla townland, Kilmacshalgan Parish, Leaffoney townland, Kilglass Parish, Coolrecuil townland, Kilmacteigue Parish, Clooneen townland, Emlyfad Parish, Cloonsillagh townland, Killaraght Parish, Rathosey townland, Killoran Parish, Stonehall townland, Ballysadare Parish, Mullafarry, Lisglennon and Newtownwhite townlands, Ballysakeery Parish.

14 In Ballysakeery, it was necessary to study three adjoining townlands (Mullafarry, Lisglennon and Newtownwhite) to achieve a representative sample. This was justifiable as it presented the only opportunity to study Presbyterian farms. In all other instances, one townland per parish was studied.

15 For a detailed account see Moffitt, 'Killala and Achonry', pp 40–9.

16 This relies on the assumption that if a farmer had a stable or coach house, he owned a horse or a coach.

17 This does not take account of the fact that a number of prosperous Roman Catholic farmers existed and that the difference from one end of the spectrum to the other was greater among Catholics than among Protestants (when the landed class are excluded.)

18 There was widespread intimidation of Protestants, and in other parts of the country the U.I.L. saw to it that ownership of their farms passed into Catholic hands, or that the larger Protestant farms were divided up. Possibly the small size of the Protestant farms in this region ensured their safety. (*S.C.* 21 March 1899, *S.C.*, 14 October 1899, *S.C.*, 21 March 1899 and *S.C.*, 14 October 1899.) *S.I.*, 8 November 1902 'Protestants and non-leaguers to be burnt down there into hell.' The same edition of this newspaper also reported the U.I.L. as saying that it wished to clear the land of grabbers, flunkies and Protestants.

19 Roll books of Mariner's school, Kilglass, County Sligo.

20 1926 was the first census to classify farm sizes and valuation according to the religion of their owners. County Laois was studied because it is roughly equal in

size to County Sligo, had an almost equal number of Protestants and was also a plantation region. However on an economic level, the land was not subdivided by the congested districts board and on a social level, it was in the middle of the wider Protestant community of the midlands unlike the marginalised Protestant community of county Sligo.

21   This is detailed in William Nolan 'Land and landscape in County Wicklow' in *Wicklow, history and society*, (Dublin, 1994) and T. Jones Hughes, 'Landholding in Meath and Cavan' in Patrick O'Flanagan, Paul Ferguson, and Kevin Whelan, (1987) *Rural Ireland, modernisation and change 1600–1900*, Cork, p. 122.

22   The 1926 census was the first to include a breakdown by age among the religious groups. After 1946 this was improved to include also a breakdown by marital status. The Church of Ireland population of County Sligo was studied to assess fertility and emigration. This does not correlate exactly to the diocese of Killala and Achonry but is the closest approximation possible.

23   Cormac Ó Gráda, *Ireland, a new economic history 1780–1939*, (Oxford, 1994) p. 221; Kurt Bowen, *Protestants in a Catholic state, Ireland's privileged minority*, (Dublin, 1983).

24   D.H. Akenson, *Small differences, Irish Catholics and Irish Protestants 1815–1922*, (Dublin:1988) p. 25. Akenson makes extensive use of Ó Gráda's study of 1700 rural families from Counties Derry and Tyrone in the 1911 census returns, see Cormac Ó Gráda, 'Did Ulster Catholics have larger families' in *Irish Economic and Social History*, xii, (1985) p. 78–80.

25   In 1946 the national average age of marriage for Roman Catholic females was 28 and for Church of Ireland females was 29.8.

26   The assumption is made that Catholic emigration occurred   for economic reasons and that where Protestant emigration   exceed Catholic emigration that social factors existed which discouraged Protestants from remaining or encouraged them to emigrate.

27   Robert E, Kennedy, jnr, *The Irish, emigration, marriage and fertility*, (London: 1973) p. 110.

28   The censuses of Ireland for the years 1926, 1936 and 1946, Parts iii and 1961,

Part v. After 1911, all official census data relates to counties and not to parishes or dioceses. For comparison purposes, the Protestant population of County Sligo is compared with the diocesan population of 1901. This is the best possible compromise, as the focus of the study is the trend of population, not the absolute population. The problem of the inclusion of an urban region in a study of rural population trends should not be ignored. The decrease in persons of 'other religions' over the years 1911–1926 in Sligo town (not in diocese) was 58.5 per cent.

29   Although the title of this thesis stipulated the years 1870–1940, the dearth of demographic data prior to 1926 necessitated a study the intercensal periods 1936–46 and 1946–61 so as to estimate the changes in the Protestant population of the region subsequent to the establishment of the Irish Free State.

30   When the term 'nation-wide' is used in a post-1926 context, it should be understood to mean throughout the 26 counties of the Irish Free State.

31   For a more thorough exploration of emigration patterns among Sligo Protestants see Moffitt, 'Killala and Achonry', pp 60–69.

32   The emigration of young children implies that families emigrated.

33   This concurs with the opinion of Donald Akenson. (Donald H. Akenson, *A mirror to Kathleen's face, education in independent Ireland, 1922–1960*, (London, 1975) p. 110.

CHURCH FINANCES

1   *I.E.G.*, 22 June 1874. Kilcommon Erris is outside the plantation zone, the other three parishes are within the plantation zone.

2   *I.E.G.*, 6 July 1894.

3   Quoted in the *Report of the Diocesan Council* for the year 1911, in the R.C.B.L., Dublin.

4   *I.E.G.*, 12 September 1885.

5   *C. of I.G.* 17 September 1920.

6   Both these parishes are inside the plantation zone.

7   Figures from *Reports to the Diocesan Synod*, in R.C.B.L., Dublin. Not all years are present, hence the approximation at a 10 yearly analysis.

8   Sir R. Palmer (£17), Owen O'Malley, Newpark Hse. (£10) both landlords and J.E.Vickery R.I.C. (£3).

9   *Report of the Diocesan Synod*, 1893, in R.C.B.L., Dublin.

10 Both Collooney and Ballysadare churches are in the single parish of Ballysadare. The parish church, St. Paul's is in the town of Collooney, Holy Trinity, a chapel of ease, is in the town of Ballysadare.

11 In some cases they continued to reside in the region and support their parish of residence but discontinued their support of the church in parishes where they had previous held land.

12 Preacher's book, Killaraght, Ms. P 204/8/1–6 in R.C.B.L., library, Dublin.

13 In 1870 there were 19 churches inside the plantation region and 9 churches outside. In 1940 there were 17 churches inside the plantation zone and one church (Straide parish, Foxford) outside.

14 An appeal for funds for Achonry parish was made in the *I.E.G.* 1 July 1879, Ballysakeery parish appealed for a scripture reader in the *I.E.G.*, 1881. Lacken parish asked for finds to repair their church in the *C.of I.G.* 25 August 1905. Foxford (Straid parish requested funds to build a glebe-house in *I.E.G.*, 3 March 1883 Kilmacshalgan asked for funds to repair their church in the *C. of I.G.* 24 September 1909. Ballysakeery parish, this appeal was published in the *I.E.G.* of 6 March 1891.

EDUCATION

1   This had ceased when the national school system was introduced.

2   The London Hibernian Society (1806), the Irish Society (1818), the Irish Church Missions (1849) were largely funded by English evangelicals, with the purpose of converting Irish Roman Catholics. Canon Macbeth, *The story of Ireland and her church*, (Dublin, 1899) pp 273–275.

3   The texts were 'Prepare to meet Thy God', 'Remember now Thy Creator in the days of thy youth', 'Have love one for another', 'Honour thy father and thy mother', 'Remember the Sabbath Day to keep it holy', 'Be not slothful in business', 'Children obey your parents in the Lord.' (N.A. ED9/252 and ED2/90/127).

4   When John McMunn, whose mother was Roman Catholic attended a national school under Roman Catholic management, his father James (Church of Ireland) had to agree in writing to his receiving Roman Catholic instruction. (N.A. ED2/90/61). When Presbyterian children attended Scurmore N.S. (under Church of Ireland management) their parents had to sign a certificate stating that they did not object to them being educated alongside Church of Ireland children (N.A. ED2/90 f.186.) The manager of Collooney school had to obtain a certificate from the parents of a Methodist pupil and give an undertaking that church catechism will not be taught to Methodist pupils in future. (N.A. ED2/66/73) The Roman Catholic mother of John Forrestal (Church of Ireland) had to present the manager of Crossmolina school with a certificate agreeing to his receiving religious instruction from a Protestant teacher (N.A.ED2/90/127).

5   Ballysadare Parish 1883, Return to Sunday School Society, in R.C.B.L., Dublin.

6   For example an appeal was made on behalf of Kilcommon Erris school in the I.E.G. on 12 February 1892.

7   Akenson, *A mirror to Kathleen's face*, pp 110–116.

8   This is the only reference to Gurraunard school, (*Report of the diocesan board of education*, 1927). There is no reference to a school in the valuation records of Gurraunard or any nearby townland.

9   Scurmore school fell out of the national system in 1890 and was maintained by the diocesan board of education in the interim. Castleconnor and Kilglass parishes had an educational endowment granted by Rev. Valentine, a former clergyman, who bequeathed £400, the interest of which was to be applied for educational purposes in the two parishes. As the needs of the church evolved, surplus money from the fund (known as the Valentine fund) was distributed to other schools in the diocese.

10 *C. of I.G.*, 25 September 1931.

11 Domestic and agricultural servants were usually local, but a cook or a butler was often from outside the diocese. (analysis of 1901 census returns).

12 N.A., ED9/29162.

13 James Greer, *The Windings of the Moy* (Ballina, Western People, 1923) 97.

14 Eric Crílís to Galway Grammar School (1936), Cecil Mac Lulis to Galway Grammar School (1932,) Máire Ní Lulis to Sligo High School (1936), Elizabeth Blakeney to Cellbridge Colliate School, Rowan Blakeney to Galway Grammar School (1928), Dorothy Blakeney to Sligo High School, Cherry Jackson to Celbridge Colliate School, Iris Jackson to Garrow School, Athlone. Mairin Ní Caimbest to Castleknock School, M. Nic Giolla Chluigeideagn to Sligo High School (1940).

INTEGRATION AND SEGREGATION

1   Rev. Walker of Emlyfad (1884–1916) was vehemently anti-Catholic. He was only a few months in charge of the parish when he re-opened the Orange Lodge, which Rev. Moore had closed over twenty years previously. [J.C. MacDonough, *Ballymote and the parish of Emlyfad* (Dublin, 1936) p166 and p. 175.
2   *C. of I.G.*, 11 July 1902.
3   *C. of I.G.*, 26 April 1912.
4   There were five Presbyterian schools in the region. The school referred to in the text was located in the village of Dromore West. (John Heuston 'The Presbyterian congregation at Dromore West, Co. Sligo, 1846– 1965' in *Irish Family History*, xiii, (1997), 76).
5   N.A., ED9/12659.
6   N.A., ED9/14595.
7   Lugawarry school was opened in December 1906 at which time there were 18 Church of Ireland children and 32 Roman Catholic children on the rolls of Lugnadiffa school.
8   N.A., ED9/18461.
9   N.A., ED9/29162.
10 N.A., ED9/18461.
11 Doobeg Hse, Bunninadden.
12 N.A., ED9/16637.
13 with the exception of Martin Stenson (Roman Catholic).
14 *S.C.,* 16 August 1890, 23 August 1890, 30 August 1890, Sept. 1890 and 18 October 1890.

15 *S.C.*, 28 May 1904.
16 *C. of I.G.*, 14 September 1923.
17 Tony Gray, *Ireland this century* (London, 1996) p. 93.
18 *S.C.*, 18 December 1880.
19 It is interesting to note that the Church of Ireland farmers in Emlyfad (Ballymote) were willing to support the Land League, regardless of their pro-landlord ultra-Protestant clergyman, Rev. Walker.
20 *S.C.*, 24 December 1880.
21 *S.C.*, 4 March 1892.
22 There were three Church of Ireland families in Lugawarry in 1901, (Black, McNiece, Morrison).
23 *S.C.*, 21 August 1880.
24 *S.C.*, 21 March 1899 and 14 October 1899.
25 *S.C.*, 25 June 1904.
26 *I.E.G.*, 8 March 1889.
27 *S.C.*, 7 June 1881.

CONCLUSION

1   Most of the 39 farms of 200+ acres probably belonged to landlords or their agents.
2   *I.E.G.*, 23 August 1889.
3   This excludes the amalgamations of Killedan with Kilconduff in 1873 and Castlemore with Killaraght in 1889. Since the populations of the resulting unions in 1901 were Kilconduff (70) and Killaraght (183) and since the parishes of Castlemore, Kilconduff and Killedan were outside the plantation region and therefore were comprised mainly of non permanent persons they were inherently non viable.
4   The Church of Ireland population of the plantation region decreased by 68.6 per cent (from 7,134 to 2,242) between 1883 and 1941, the Church of Ireland population of the rest of the diocese decreased by 89.6 per cent (from 623 to 66) over the same period.
5   1941 population, (*Report of the Diocesan Synod*, 1941, in R.C.B.L., Dublin).